DUBLIN
THE STORY OF A CITY

First published 2016 by The O'Brien Press Ltd,

12 Terenure Road East, Rathgar, Dublin 6, D06 HD27, Ireland.

Tel: +353 1 4923333; Fax: +353 1 4922777

E-mail: books@obrien.ie

Website: www.obrien.ie

The O'Brien Press is a member of Publishing Ireland.

Hardcover ISBN: 978-1-84717-813-8

Limited slipcase edition ISBN: 978-1-84717-922-7

Artwork of the Custom House, Dublin, commissioned by Jacqueline O'Brien.

Endpapers: panorama of the River Liffey and Central Dublin in 1988, commissioned by The O'Brien Press.

1 3 5 7 9 10 8 6 4 2

16 18 20 19 17

Layout and design: The O'Brien Press Ltd.

Printed in Drukarnia Skleniarz, Poland.

The paper used in this book is produced using pulp from managed forests.

Published in

DUBLIN
UNESCO
City of Literature

Dedication

To the many generations of Dubliners

who have made the city the remarkable place that it is today.

Acknowledgements

SC: I was delighted to hear from Michael and Ivan O'Brien that they wished to publish a collection of my drawings of Dublin and to commission new ones for this book. Peter Harbison was the first choice as writer, and he has responded to the drawings in a very positive way. Over the years I have consulted many specialists, including Professor Howard B. Clarke, Professor Roger Stalley, Dr Edward McParland, Mr Conleth Manning, Professor Ian Campbell Ross and Dr Stuart Kinsella, who gave freely of their time to advise and comment on the work in progress. I have benefited greatly from images in the collections of the Irish Architectural Archive. For specific requests, I wish to thank Ms Ciara Kerrigan, Assistant Keeper in the Office of the Chief Herald, Ms Sharon Lynch of WK Nowlan REIT Management Ltd, Ms Nuala Reilly of Irish Waterways, Ms Lisa Ward and Ms Jennifer O'Loughlin of Grant Thornton. The staff of The O'Brien Press have made this work a pleasure, combining efficiency with imagination.

PH: When Michael O'Brien invited me to write the main text to accompany Stephen Conlin's splendid pictures for this book, I jumped at the opportunity, because I was in awe at the quality of Stephen's artwork. My main thanks, therefore, are primarily due to Stephen and Michael for the pleasure of working with them, but also to Nicola Reddy, who did a remarkable job editing, and Emma Byrne, for a beautiful design. Most importantly, I also want to express my gratitude to the authors listed in the selected bibliography at the back of the book, whose works I have consulted with great benefit, and whose knowledge I have been happy to include in the creation of my text.

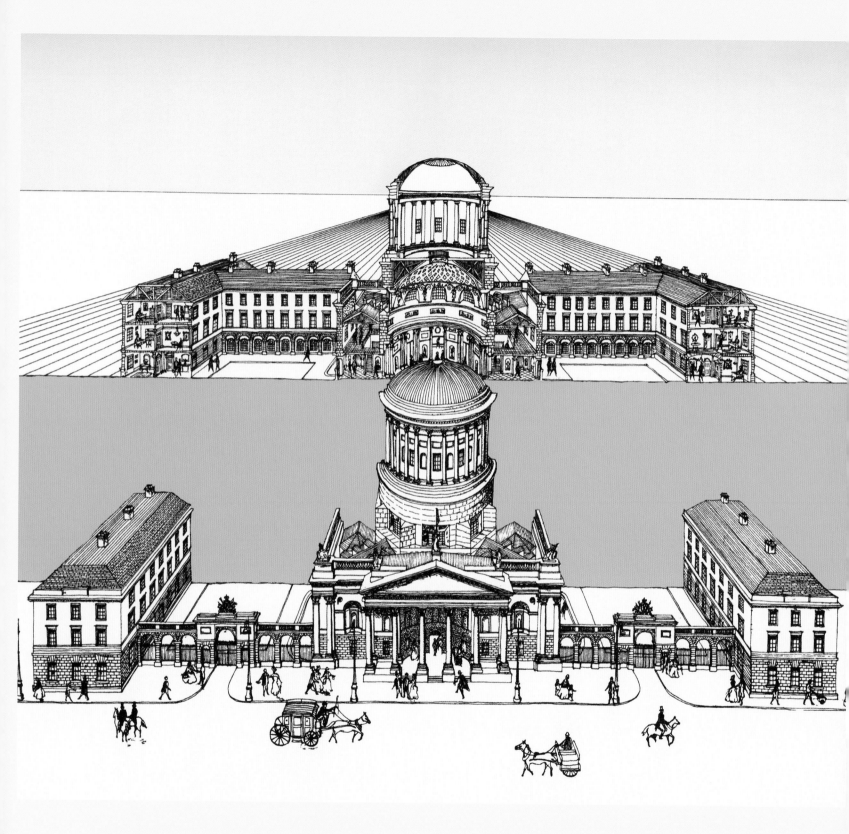

THE FOUR COURTS, DESIGNED IN 1786 BY JAMES GANDON (1743–1823). PERSPECTIVE STUDY WITH CUT-AWAY INTERIOR.

DUBLIN
THE STORY OF A CITY

Illustrations and additional text by

STEPHEN CONLIN

Main text by

PETER HARBISON

THE O'BRIEN PRESS
DUBLIN

CONTENTS

THE IRISH HOUSES OF PARLIAMENT, BEGUN IN 1729 AND SHOWN HERE *CIRCA* 1760.

ARCHITECT SIR EDWARD LOVETT PEARCE (1699–1733). SEE P.81.

INTRODUCTION

I f you go up the Dublin Mountains south-west of the city, in the area around Killakee, and look down over the Liffey 'delta' spreading out before you, you see a sprawling conurbation of over a million people, which is a far cry from what you would have seen a thousand years ago. Where the city now spreads out in suburbs heading for Dún Laoghaire and Howth, back then there was only a small settlement in the centre. Its denizens had just engaged in the Battle of Clontarf in 1014, which did not, despite popular belief, rid Ireland of the Vikings. They continued on, and DNA would doubtless show that their blood still flows in Dubliners' veins.

These Norsemen had arrived a century and a half earlier, mainly from Norway, and established a trading post on the banks of the River Liffey. They were ousted by the native Irish, who had what would seem to have been a monastery in the area around Stephen Street, but the Norsemen returned around 917 to found a permanent settlement on the spur of land enclosing Dublin Castle and Christ Church Cathedral. That was the real beginning of the city as it now stands, despite claims hailed in a spurious millennium celebration in 1988!

In time, Dublin was conquered by the Vikings' remote cousins, the Normans, in 1170 and given to the men of Bristol two years later. From then until 1922, Dublin Castle — which grew out of an earlier Norse fortification found beneath it — became the centre of Norman and then English power in Ireland.

Probably more than the inhabitants of any other city in Europe, Dubliners have gone through a number of languages in the course of their history: Gaelic, Old Norse, Norman French and English, the last having become the norm during the past two hundred years. With such a linguistic change, one might almost have expected the citizens to have developed a language of their own, with local idioms and vocabulary, yet this has not manifested itself greatly. What Dubliners do have, however, is a generosity of syllables, employing two where one could do, or making two become three. The best example is the name of the city itself, pronounced 'Dubbel-in', divided by the River Liffey into two sides, 'de nort sigh-yed' and 'de sout sigh-yed'. One often hears outsiders speak of the Dublin accent, but the fact of the matter is that there are myriad accents, depending on locality and social status. There is even a moving one, the 'DART accent', as spoken by those who travel on the suburban train service – Dublin Area Rapid Transit – which runs right around Dublin Bay.

But perhaps the change of languages helped to loosen Dubliners' tongues, for they are great talkers. The 'gift of the gab' is said to be best practised in pubs, but it is probably more common nowadays in the cafés that have sprung up like mushrooms all over the city. This linguistic dexterity also spawned a literature for which Dublin is famous – Swift in the eighteenth century, Le Fanu, Stoker and Wilde among others in the nineteenth, with Joyce and Beckett dominating the twentieth. Indeed, Joyce's *Ulysses*, published in 1922, placed the map of Dublin on the world's literary stage by describing in the most evocative colours the workings of a city and its people on one particular day in 1904.

Not to be forgotten in this context is the exhilarating theatre life of the city, going back to the Smock Alley Theatre in the seventeenth century, Sheridan in the eighteenth, with Wilde, Shaw, O'Casey and others sharing the nineteenth and twentieth centuries between them. Their works and those of Irish and foreign playwrights are often presented on the boards of the Abbey and Gate theatres, but also in smaller and more intimate venues.

The throbbing life of any city is the constant interaction between its citizens and the street-side buildings – and what goes on inside them. It is worth noting that Dublin's two cathedrals, Christ Church and St. Patrick's, and the nearby church of St. Audoen's, are really the only medieval buildings still surviving above ground in the old parts of the city, and that, of course, is because they were built of stone. For some two-thirds of Dublin's existence, its population lived in structures of wattle and wood, which have long since vanished and can be reconstructed only on the basis of archaeological excavation. It was not until around 1700 that brick came into its own as the staple building material of Dublin's houses, and it was the chosen medium of the eighteenth and nineteenth centuries, enhancing the beauty of the squares and streets that adorn the city centre and beyond. Times have now changed considerably, and the concrete block is much more the staple diet, perhaps less attractive as a material but enabling the construction of grander and taller architectural creations which also facilitate more internal light than was ever possible or conceivable before.

Dublin's history is like a yo-yo, going up and down over the centuries, and its buildings often help to reflect the changes that have taken place over time. Not all the city is beautiful; financial upheavals have caused restrictions of building activity and even dereliction, with deplorable gaps occurring, but have left the really great public structures and central squares with their eye-popping doorways largely intact.

Stephen Conlin's beautifully crafted illustrations in this volume overlook those parts of the city described as 'dear dirty Dublin' and concentrate on a remarkable selection of areas and individual buildings which truly give us an insight into the see-saw of architectural development of the city, from Viking cabins to Norman/English half-timbered houses, from cathedrals to grandiose Georgian buildings, nineteenth-century houses and churches, and ending up with some of the best of twentieth-century architecture in the city and its environs. Walking along Dublin's streets, we see the façades of the buildings that flank us – but it takes the brush and pen strokes of a master watercolourist and draughtsman like Stephen Conlin to make us see the larger patterns, by providing us with an intriguingly detailed and animated bird's-eye view of the city, which none of those new-fangled drones would ever be able to recreate, let alone copy or imitate.

Peter Harbison, 2016

THE CUSTOM HOUSE, BEGUN IN 1781 AND SHOWN HERE CIRCA 1840. ARCHITECT JAMES GANDON (1743–1823). SEE P. 117.

FOREWORD

This book explores how Dublin came to be the European capital it is today, a destination for people from all over the world who want to find out more about Irish culture and history. Yet the city has within it many strands: we see a Scandinavian town, linked by kinship to Norway; then a medieval town that formed part of a Norman sphere of influence covering a large part of Western Europe; and, by the eighteenth century, a 'polite' city, with entertainments at which musicians of international reputation performed the latest works. The aim of my drawings is to recreate these times, and also to celebrate more recognisable views for the quality of the urban fabric.

Reconstruction drawings, when the past has been swept away, present a challenge in trying to visualise what was once the daily life of Dubliners. The tension here is between evidence and speculation. Decades ago, it would have been difficult to obtain information about how places looked; architectural historians and archaeologists were justifiably focused on the standing stones and fragments that had come to light. Trying to work out how a medieval building was roofed is still a difficult question. While it is laudable to stay strictly with the evidence, there has been a move in recent years to present historical sites in a more engaging and accessible way. I have been encouraged in my work by many specialists who have given their time to help to recreate Dublin's past.

Most drawings start with a plan, in order to see how the land lies. This is traditional perspective work: intersecting lines are drawn across the page from vanishing points, usually located off the paper to the right and left. The plan is then added to the drawing, using a system of squares. This all helps to hold the drawing together, although there are naturally many variations in a scene, and not everything will conform to the grid. Most work needs some adjustment by eye to make it more satisfying.

Once the buildings have been projected up according to their likely scale, it's now necessary to 'clothe' them. For this stage, contemporary drawings, engravings and paintings can supply a huge amount of information. For example, Thomas Burgh's library in Trinity College, Dublin, went through several changes that are visible in paintings and engravings. At first, it had an open, arcaded ground floor with two sand-coloured upper floors, then the roofline changed around 1860 when the wooden barrel vault was added to the Long Room. Finally, the ground floor was enclosed in the 1890s.

Having added these details to the buildings, it's time to show the drawing to specialists who can comment on the appearance of landmarks and the drawing as a whole. After consultation and amendments, the linework is added in coloured inks, often grey and sepia. Watercolour and some colour pencil work, and finally the effect of shadow, bring the piece to completion.

For parts of the city that have not changed too much,

a good viewing point may be the start of a drawing. To evoke Dublin along the Liffey in the 1950s (p. 188), I used the viewing point of Liberty Hall, then removed later buildings and replaced them. For the modern view of Trinity College from over Westland Row (p. 204), I used aerial photography and was given access to a nearby tall building; likewise for the image of the Liffey looking east (p. 230). Online digital maps and aerial photography provide resources undreamt of a few years ago. It's now possible to check rooflines, windows and chimneys from various angles in the pursuit of accuracy – and it can be done from a computer anywhere in the world. That coverage is part of a bigger picture.

In a matter of decades, Dublin has linked itself fully to the modern world. If people in the 1950s feared that Ireland would be increasingly cut off by its geographical position and economic situation, they were luckily proved wrong. Since the 1970s, there has been a renaissance: Dublin has taken its place as a European capital, thanks to economic advances, education, and the freedom to travel. Dubliners have come to see the value of Georgian buildings, and in spite of the losses in the twentieth century, the city still possesses fine streets, squares and handsome buildings, places that Oscar Wilde and James Joyce knew. Visitors to Europe now have Dublin in their sights as a significant cultural centre, whether they have Irish blood or not.

The drawings in this book show many stages in the

city's development, including how it outgrew the walled town and expanded to become a focus of Georgian life, both bustling and gracious; they show the quality of Dublin's built environment today, and how it is valuing the past while building new structures. What has come down to us is a national treasure. This collection of pictures —

complemented and enhanced by the engaging and informative words of Peter Harbison — came about through the encouragement of the publisher Michael O'Brien. The book celebrates the many forms of Dublin through the centuries.

Stephen Conlin, 2016

PUBLISHER'S NOTE

This project has its beginnings in the mid-1980s when, following an appeal for new illustration talent, I came across Stephen Conlin and his beautiful architectural reconstruction drawings.

In 1986, I first proposed to Stephen a book called *Dublin Recreated*, which would show the city emerging over a thousand-year period. The inspiration came partly from my own experience occupying the medieval/Viking archaeological site at Wood Quay to protest the shameful destruction of Dublin's heritage. F.X. Martin, acclaimed cleric, historian and the activist who led the massive protests in 1978 and 1979, agreed to write the text for the book, and Stephen went to work on the drawings. With F.X. unable to find the time, in 1988 we published a stopgap — *Dublin, One Thousand Years* — with both text and illustration by Stephen.

Years passed, yet the dream of a major book persisted. In 2014, Stephen agreed to add significant new artwork, both enlarging the scope of the book and highlighting the many positive changes to Dublin's landscape. We asked Peter Harbison, renowned historian, to write the accompanying text, to which he has brought his unique experience and distinct style.

In fact, the postponed publication has proved a blessing — now we can show a renewed Dublin through Peter's skilfully chosen words and Stephen's exceptional drawings of the Samuel Beckett Bridge, the Convention Centre, the inspiring Grand Canal Dock development, the rebirth of Smithfield, and much more. Thirty years later, our dream has finally come true.

Michael O'Brien, 2016

VIK
COL

ING
ONY

VIKING DUBLIN

owadays, we consider Dublin a wonderful place to live from a recreational point of view, with a sea to swim in and hills to climb. When the Vikings arrived in Dublin Bay in the first half of the ninth century, they must have been reminded of their homeland – namely modern-day Norway, where Oslo has similar facilities. In the splendid keeled and clinker-built boats they had developed – like the *Oseberg* and *Gokstad* vessels one can see in the Viking Ship Museum in western Oslo today – they had the ability to sail far distances across the North Sea to Scotland, the Faroes, Iceland, Greenland and beyond, but also to Ireland, where they first landed in the year 795.

Some were farmers looking for more and better land than what they had back home, where they could raise a family, for in time they would have brought their wives with them. But others had treasure on their minds; not buried treasure, but booty to be got by raiding rich settlements and, in the case of Ireland, monasteries, with their decorative crosses and reliquaries. Some of these items were brought back to Norway and either sold or given to spouses or relatives, with whom the objects (or parts of them) were often buried. It is not surprising, therefore, that some of the finest specimens of Irish monastic metalwork are to be found in the museums of Norway, having been dug up from graves discovered during the last century and a half. Some reliquary caskets may have reached Scandinavia by trade, for the Vikings were intrepid travellers in the interest of commerce, going as far as Constantinople. From there, they brought back exotic silks – these have been found in the Dublin city excavations within the last fifty years — and also silver coins, which have been found in considerable numbers in various locations around Ireland.

A small Irish monastery that may have been one of the first to draw the attention of the Viking raiders can be seen as a circular area in the centre left of the picture, just above the cluster of boats. The round shape was created by an earthen bank surrounding the monks' oratory and huts, and that same curvature can still be traced over a thousand years later in the bend of Stephen Street in the city today. It is close to what was once a dark pool, *Dubh Linn* in Irish, which gave the capital one of its earliest names. Fed by the River Poddle but now filled in, it was in the angle created today by the south side of Dublin Castle and the Chester Beatty Library. It was in this pool that the Vikings would have moored — and probably repaired — their boats after long and tedious voyages, but only after they had decided to settle in Dublin in 841, and to make it a raiding and trading base.

What, you may well ask, were the Vikings doing between their first Irish landing (probably on Rathlin Island, County Antrim) in 795 and their making a permanent settlement at the confluence of the rivers Poddle and Liffey in 841? They may well have had some less permanent settlement farther upriver near what is now Kilmainham, because that is where a number of Viking graves — some from at least the first half of the ninth century — were discovered when railway tracks were being laid out westwards from what is now Heuston Station in the 1840s. These burials contained swords, indicating warriors, brooches belonging to their high-status wives, and also weighing scales, revealing that traders, too, must have been interred there. Hitherto, no settlement has been found to accompany these grave-goods, suggesting that this location may have been more of a trading depot and, more particularly, a base from which the Vikings could have made raids. That is, indeed, the pattern that we find recorded in the old Irish Annals, in which their monastic compilers pointed out to the world the devastation which these Northern raiders were causing among the monasteries of the time — those same raids in which the metalwork was being pillaged and taken back to Norway. It was these Annals that gave the Vikings such a bad press as murderers and looters; that is, until the danger of destruction of important parts of Dublin made the people of Ireland realise that the Vikings had also contributed significantly to our way of life through introducing coinage (in 997), boatbuilding techniques, and instituting markets (the Irish word for which, *margadh*, is of Norse origin). Such developments did not happen overnight, but over the centuries the Norsemen integrated well with the local population, getting their foodstuffs, wood, animals and sometimes their wives from them. In time, too, many of them would have become proficient in talking Irish so that the city gradually became bilingual, with Norse and Gaelic being spoken side by side around the year 1000.

But this is rather to run ahead of the story. So let us go back again to the early ninth century, a phase when the Vikings were making hasty 'hit-and-run' raids on Irish monasteries, as recorded in the Annals, and speedily retreating to their ships with whatever booty they were able to grab. However, the time came when they found this method of warring not entirely satisfactory and decided to found some permanent settlements. One of the first was at Annagassan in County Louth, just north of the Boyne, where they settled in 840. It took only one year for them to realise the strategic benefits of Dublin, farther south – a well-sheltered area along the banks of the Liffey where they could moor their boats in the quiet Poddle pool of *Dubh Linn*, and where a raised ridge on the south bank of the Liffey gave them a good view of any potential marauders (and there were some) who might want to attack their cargo, which was tied up along a makeshift quay, as seen in the bottom of the main picture. For intrepid navigators who knew their marine geography, Dublin was an ideal port for the Vikings' escapades. Looking at a map of the whole sea-façade of Western Europe, Dublin is a kind of halfway house between Scandinavia and the Iberian Peninsula; this helped it to become one of the Norsemen's most important depots and trading centres in these islands, the Irish equivalent of York in the north of England. In addition to animal hides, slaves were undoubtedly an important trading commodity. The Icelandic *Laxdaela Saga* has a touching account of the daughter of an Irish king who was sold as a

THE FIRST SETTLEMENT

The higher ground now occupied by Dublin Castle would also have been of defensive interest to early Viking settlers, given its view out over the surrounding territory, and their first encampment would have been in this area. Later building has removed almost all traces of the Viking stronghold, but we see here the type of timber hall that would have served for meetings: this is based on archaeological research in the Scandinavian home countries. Above the cleared area in front of the hall is just visible, beyond the defences, a remarkable survival from Gaelic Dublin: the round tower of St. Michael-le-Pole. It was over twenty-seven metres high and stood until 1776.

We see here Viking boats being repaired in the dark pool – *Dubh Linn* in Irish – from which the city takes its name. This area would have provided extra protection from the elements, and the flat-bottomed boats could have been brought easily from the Liffey for extensive maintenance. The River Poddle, which fed the pool, was later diverted and the ground dried out to become the garden of Dublin Castle. The area just above the boats, enclosed by trees and shrubs, indicates the Gaelic monastic enclosure that is still partly evident in the street plan of Dublin, along Stephen Street.

slave in Oslo and brought to Iceland, where she bore her master a boy; he later went by the lovely name of Olaf the Peacock. The Irish and the Scots played an important role in the early gene pool of the Icelandic population.

Smaller items would also have been traded, as revealed by the excavations in Old Dublin some decades ago. Particularly popular were bone combs, of which hundreds survive, leatherwork for shoes and knife-sheaths. Much rarer were sculptures of wood, some decorated with beautiful animal ornament of a kind practised back in Scandi-navia and among the Vikings who had settled in considerable numbers in England, north and south.

The settlement created by the Vikings in Dublin would have been called a *longphort*, really a permanent base for raiding. This activity did not stop with settling down in a permanent home but went on intermittently until 880, after which four decades of comparative peace reigned in Ireland. Relations with the kings of the surrounding countryside, Leinster and Mide in particular, were often bellicose, and the Irish regularly proved superior in battle during the ninth century. But, at other times, those same Gaelic lords provided useful alliances for the Dublin Vikings, when the latter's mercenary forces would have fought with one Irish king against another, as was the case in the famous Battle of Clontarf in 1014.

Even before the Vikings arrived in Dublin, there had been an important river ford at the lowest crossable location at low tide on the River Liffey; it helped to join south Dublin and Wicklow with north Dublin and Meath and provided the normal name for Dublin nowadays – *Áth Cliath*, 'the ford of the hurdle-work'. North Dublin is now called Fingal, 'the land of the fair foreigners', after the Norwegians who had settled in the region as far north as Skerries. Some Scandinavian place-names still survive there, such as Holmpatrick, Lambay and even Skerries itself, though the houses where these people lived have yet to be discovered. The name Leixlip, from the Norse for 'salmon-leap', shows that they also stretched out westwards as far as County Kildare.

The Viking *longphort* would have lasted until the first few years of the tenth century, and only recently have some burials come to light in the Temple Bar area that would have belonged to the inhabitants of Old Dublin at the time. In 902, a powerful Irish force drove the Vikings out

TRADE EXPANSION

Viking traders, with their specialised boats, would have found the shore of the Liffey ideal for tying up to load and unload their goods, which might have included slaves. At the time when this image is set, around the year 975, the river would have been much wider and shallower; we are seeing it before the gradual reclamation of ground that took place in the Anglo-Norman period. The curving line of Fishamble Street is suggested on the right here, near the area excavated at the time of the Wood Quay controversy in the 1970s (see p. 38).

of Dublin, whereupon they retreated to England and Scotland — but only for a decade and a half, as they returned with renewed vigour in 917 to remain there for centuries. The bulk of what we see reconstructed on pp. 18–19 is not the *longphort* of the ninth century but the beginning of a town developing in the tenth century. The idea of founding a town is one that the Vikings may well have learned during their years of 'exile' in England.

Obviously, the town of Dublin would have started with small beginnings, like the proverbial mustard seed, but gradually the settlement grew to cover much of the ridge later to be occupied by Dublin Castle and Christ Church Cathedral. Individuals doubtless squabbled to get the best kind of holdings for themselves, as the land available dictated that only a small amount of space could be allotted to each family. Plots of land would probably have been handed down from one generation to the next, and we know of at least one instance where a house was taken down and replaced on the same spot up to thirteen times. This, of course, implies that houses were made of perishable materials that would last only for a certain length of time, and it would not be unreasonable to suppose that a house would have had to have been replaced once every fifteen or twenty years.

Viking houses were of two main kinds. The larger house type was four and a half metres long, with walls of wattle interwoven with upright posts. Inside, in the centre, upright beams in a square supported a thatched roof with a chimney opening above. For sitting and sleeping, there were raised areas around the hearth in the centre of the house. The wattle would have had some mud added to keep out the draught, but a door at each end must have allowed the occasional breeze to waft through. The other house type was smaller, also wattled and thatched but with only a single door, which would have made for a dark and smoky interior (the fire was kept lit not just in winter but possibly throughout the year to provide cooking and cleaning facilities). An outline of the plans of the two house types has been imaginatively inserted among the modern pebbled paving on the eastern side of Winetavern Street, below Christ Church Cathedral, for anyone interested in establishing their size.

The larger houses at least would have had a small green space in front of them, with an even smaller area at the back, where the cess-pit for human waste would have been located. Between the houses were wooden-paved streets, some probably ill-drained and containing human and animal refuse, doubtless creating smells that modern noses would find difficult to bear. We know little of wells, but likely it is that they were present to provide water. Somewhere, too, there must have been a central meeting place, which the picture suggests may have been beneath the later Dublin Castle. Here, too, the elders and organisers could trade and administer and allocate housing plots, among other things. Beyond the southern boundary of the nascent town, we can see the River Poddle, which rose above Tallaght and, before being partially re-routed in the late twelfth century, passed through the *Dubh Linn* and around two sides of Dublin Castle before entering the Liffey at the north-eastern corner of the settlement.

In the tenth century, there would have been an earthen bank, probably with a wooden palisade on top, to act as a defence. This served not only to keep undesirables out but also to keep animals in, as cows, sheep and pigs may have been kept to provide meat for the inhabitants and bone for the craftsmen.

A VIKING WOMAN

A Viking woman of this period could enjoy certain privileges, such as inheriting and owning property in her own right. In this picture, she has the blonde hair that would have struck the native Irish when they first saw these strangers who had come to stay. She is making yarn with carded wool, which is wrapped round the wooden distaff in her left hand. Hanging from her right hand is a spindle stick, weighted with a stone whorl at its base in the centre of her apron dress. The woman sets the spindle stick in motion at her chosen speed, feeding the carded wool to create the yarn, which builds up as she works. They were other methods of Viking yarn-making, but the principle was always the same.

The 1970s excavations revealed evidence of the status of Viking women, including a silk scarf and hairnets, which were remarkable finds. The special conditions at Wood Quay were of international significance and provided an insight into the daily life of a thousand years before. Our subject here owns some decoration in the form of a necklace and the brooches that are used to secure her apron dress, which may have been of linen.

In the twelfth century, Dublin changed from being Viking, or Hiberno-Norse, to Norman, all the while developing from what was a small conglomeration of huts into what may be realistically described as a town. Dublin's power might have weakened after the Battle of Clontarf in 1014, but its wealth increased to such an extent that, throughout the eleventh century, the Irish realised that it was Dublin — rather than the traditional High Kingship of Tara — that was the prize worth fighting for in Ireland. Both secularly and in religion, Dublin was integrating more and more into the Irish scene, and, after the middle of the eleventh century, Irish kings succeeded the Norse as rulers of Dublin. It was probably they who reinforced the defences around 1100 by replacing an earlier earthen wall with a stone one; this was to be strengthened again after the arrival of the Normans in the early 1170s. They were the warriors who built a castle at the south-eastern corner of the defences, and from it northwards and westwards stretched their town wall, enclosing an area of forty-four acres, full of houses, streets and bustling life.

Those fighting on the parapets during a siege would have been protected by archers standing on the taller towers dotted along the course of the walls. Only those towers that formed part of the castle still survive, but in time, over a dozen such towers came to be built — one of which is seen in the bottom left of the main picture. The walls required a lot of stone, which would have been quarried outside the town's boundaries, probably in the foothills of the Dublin Mountains. They are seen in the background slightly enveloped in rain. Up to about 1250, the climate was probably much as it is today, though snow and ice may have been a little more prevalent in winter. After the middle of the thirteenth century, it became rather more damp, making life difficult for Irish farmers in the surrounding countryside and necessitating more wood for the fires in Dublin houses. These would no longer have been the wattle-and-daub structures of the Viking period but rectangular houses with a framework of stout timber beams, with lighter beams and wattle in between.

By the Later Middle Ages, the population of Dublin would have enlarged somewhat. During the Viking period, it was probably less than five thousand, but with trade, increasing production and the (sometimes dubious) advantages of city life, the number would have expanded considerably by the fourteenth century. We may glorify the Middle Ages as the age of chivalry, with knights in shining armour jousting on horseback, but for ordinary urban folk, life must have been rather different. None of the electric lights, running water, sanitation or central heating that we have today; in comparison, town life in the medieval period must have been rather squalid. There was one elementary supply of water to the city, but to get it home, you would have had to fetch it in a bucket or pail. Some people had a cess-pit in their back garden, but the narrow streets would have stank with the smell of animal offal disposed of by irresponsible butchers, probably in the middle of the night.

Most of the foodstuffs were probably supplied from outside the city walls. We know that rotund friars and higher clerics would have been getting their three good meals a day, with pork, lamb or beef regularly on the menu. But the common man and woman had a much reduced selection on their wooden plates. Many would have wandered out into the countryside to pick berries and nuts, and the grave of one individual showed that his last meal consisted of what were virtually weeds – knot grass and goosefoot. But, being near the sea, marine products such as fish, oysters, cockles and mussels (of Molly Malone fame) would also have been on offer, while the urban housewife would probably have had a small pen for poultry in her back yard. However, life was grim when famine struck, as it did occasionally during the Middle Ages. The year 1317 (when the Bruce invasion threatened Dublin) was particularly bad; some soldiers, we are told, even raided cemeteries and ate the recent dead. In 1295, hunger had forced others to eat the corpses of those hanging on the gallows. For the Hiberno-Norse inhabitants, the earlier conquest of the town by the Normans must have seemed mild in comparison.

These Normans were, in essence, the descendants (collateral or otherwise) of the same Vikings who founded Dublin in 841. They had harried and made life so difficult for the French king, Charles the Simple, that they were able to force him in 911 to give them land in northern France, which, understandably, became known as Normandy. From there it was but a step across the English

Channel for William the Conqueror to subjugate Anglo-Saxon England in 1066. A century later, it was the enticement of inheriting the province of Leinster by marrying the daughter of its king, Dermot MacMurrough, that encouraged one of the English king's barons, Richard de Clare, Earl of Pembroke (better known as Strongbow) to cross the Irish Sea and try his luck at conquering at least parts of Ireland. When his wife died in 1171, he took over Leinster. The Norman invaders had first taken control of the Viking cities of Wexford and Waterford, and now Dublin was in their sights. At that time, the town was ruled by a Hiberno-Norse king, Asculf, but his forces were defeated by the better-equipped Normans. Asculf

retreated to Britain and later returned with the intention of regaining his kingdom, but was again vanquished by the Normans, who, when he defied them, chopped off his head in reprisal.

One of Asculf's allies was Rory O'Connor, King of Connacht, who was also outwitted by the Norman invaders and failed to realise the danger their arrival meant for the stability of the whole country. But Strongbow had another king to deal with, namely his own, Henry II of England, who spent much of his life in France trying to keep his kingdom together on both sides of the English Channel. Henry began to worry that Strongbow was gaining too much power and might at any moment set himself up as

WALLS OF STONE

Dublin Castle is seen on the right in this inset, where the Viking hall was shown in the previous chapter. The town walls are now of stone and provide a convincing deterrent for any force. A small church, St. Mary del Dam, stands just in front of the leftmost tower of the castle, which looks out over the marshy ground that used to be the black pool, *Dubh Linn*. The River Poddle that fed the pool still flows to this day, now in a culvert, and its confluence with the River Liffey can be seen at Wellington Quay at low water. Gaelic remains take the form of the round tower of St. Michael-le-Pole, seen on the extreme top right, and the monastic enclosure, top left, which by this point was regaining its religious significance with the Church of St. Peter.

Sturdy houses were built within the walls below Christ Church Cathedral, while outside, on the shoreline, warehouses sprang up to store the goods being traded between Ireland and several other countries. The characteristic course of the city wall is seen here, wending its way across what was to be an important excavation site in the 1970s. The River Liffey is being pushed back by wooden revetments with backfilling, to create greater draft for boats; in the next chapter, we'll see how successive reclamations will regain a stretch of land from the river to permit the building of a stone quay.

monarch of some parts of Ireland. Henry decided that he had better clip Strongbow's wings, and he set out to conquer Ireland himself, in person. There, he received the fealty not only of Dublin but also of a number of Irish kings, whereupon Strongbow retreated to Wales, from whence he had come.

It was at this juncture that King Henry II gave Dublin to the men of Bristol, a town in the south-west of England that was probably smaller than Dublin at the time. But why Bristol? This town near the Severn mouth had been building up its trade around the Irish Sea during the eleventh century but was still playing second fiddle to Dublin's dominance. Its good pottery was exported to Dublin, where it has been found in quantities in the Old Dublin excavations. To be given control of its trading rival was a great

boost for the Bristolians, but a grave disappointment to the Dubliners. One of the reasons why Henry II favoured the men of Bristol was that he had spent a part of his youth not far from the town, and he was happy to give them some benefit from his most recent conquest across the Irish Sea.

Christ Church Cathedral, seen in the extreme right of the main picture, was an important focus in Norman Dublin and brings us to consider the religious change that had come about during the course of the eleventh century. In the ninth and tenth centuries, the Norse gods of Odin and Thor would have been Dublin's dominant deities, but around the turn of the millennium the Christian religion was making strides in converting the population to its tenets. One of Dublin's kings, Sitric, went on a pilgrimage to Rome in the second quarter of the eleventh century. So impressed was he that he founded a church on his return, probably with the assistance of a bishop named Dúnán. This happened around 1030, and in 1152, the church was raised to cathedral status. Nothing remains of it now, but in its place the Normans started to build the present Christ Church Cathedral in a Romanesque style around 1180. It was provided with a crypt – the only church in the country ever to have a crypt running underneath most of its length.

By the year 1200, the cathedral was beginning to make its mark on the skyline, with the aid of masons and sculptors brought from the west of England, together with an easily workable oolite stone from a quarry at Dundry, not far from Bristol. It was finished in the Gothic style by the end of the thirteenth century. Even before it was built, the site had been in the hands of the Augustinian Canons, at the instigation of St. Laurence O'Toole, an archbishop of Dublin who died in 1180. Within the railings south of the building, there still exist traces of the chapter house, where the canons would have sat to hear their abbot speak and to recite the scriptures, but the rest of the monastery's buildings were demolished centuries ago.

In 1562, the roof and south wall of the nave collapsed, after which decay set in. But the cathedral was restored in 1872–1878 by the architect George Edmund Street, with generous financial help from Henry Roe, a rich Dublin distiller who almost bankrupted himself in the process. Christ Church remained the most important religious structure within the city's walls during the Middle Ages, but there were other smaller churches too, including St. Audoen's, not far away, whose patron came from Rouen in northern France, suggesting that it was a Norman foundation.

ST. PATRICK'S CATHEDRAL

St. Patrick's rises on low-lying ground near the course of the River Poddle. It is an ambitious structure, the largest in Ireland, and would have impressed Dubliners with its scale when construction started after 1191. Here it is seen with the frozen Poddle receding into the distance. At this stage, in 1275, work has started on a tower, but this will be rebuilt in 1362–1370 and again in 1394. It is called Minot's Tower, named after the Archbishop of Dublin who oversaw the work.

A MEDIEVAL TRADER

This man is a wealthy trader from Norman times. He may well be descended from the original Bristolians who found rich pickings following King Henry II's 'donation' of Dublin to the men of Bristol. We can imagine that he owns several ships that bring goods from overseas — he may have brought the stone from Dundry in Somerset to build Christ Church Cathedral. He is dressed in an expensive lined coat and has his left hand on a coloured leather purse. Evidence of leather shoes and fabrics has been excavated from this period.

WOOD QUAY

The arrival of the Normans, along with King Henry II's handing over the city to his beloved men of Bristol in 1172, was to bring about a momentous change in Dublin, which a royal charter was to make into a capital city. Perhaps the least change was seen in the pattern of thoroughfares such as Fishamble Street, which had been created by the Hiberno-Norse inhabitants centuries earlier; these remain much the same today. In contrast, little remains of the northern section of the Hiberno-Norse city wall of stone seen here wending its way right across the centre of the picture. It has two curious angular bends; these may have been caused by a desire to build on stable bedrock, or perhaps the wall was following the line of some earlier barrier that kept the river — and those who might sail up it to attack — at bay.

The stone wall had been erected around 1100, as a defence for a town whose prestige and trading potential was being realised more and more. The Normans, when they came, however, needed to allow soldiers and merchants access to the town, and for this reason, they added guarded gates. One of these was King's Gate at the top of Winetavern Street, which served those coming up from what may have been a small slip or mooring inlet close to the river. On the right of the picture is a further strong gate, Mac Giolla Mo-Cholmoc's. Unusually, it was called after a local Gaelic chieftain, whose strength must have been sufficiently respected by the Norman invaders for them to have allowed his name to have been commemorated in this fashion.

One way in which the Norman overlords were seen to dominate their new city, both physically and spiritually, was through ecclesiastical structures that arose along the higher ground above Wood Quay. Most noteworthy among them was Christ Church Cathedral, mentioned in the previous chapter, which forms the centrepiece on the horizon here. Around 1180, the Bristolians started with the choir, for which they brought over sculptors from the west of England to carve the decorative capitals, some of which still survive. By the early thirteenth century, further masons were imported to construct the tower and nave of the cathedral, which vied with the pure Early English style of St. Patrick's Cathedral, seen under construction in the image on p. 36.

Another church that went back to a Hiberno-Norse foundation was St. Olaf's (or Olave's), presumably named after a Norwegian king. It was located along Fishamble Street, on the left of the picture, but it disappeared centuries ago, as did St. John's, seen here to the left of Christ Church, with the red roof. Old St. Audoen's on High Street is the only medieval church (as opposed to cathedral) surviving in the city. Although thought by some to have been founded by the Vikings, its origins are much more likely to lie with the Normans, as the name of its dedicatee probably comes from Normandy in northern France, home to the Normans from 911. Another Norman church in the locality was St. Michael's, whose tower is visible to the right of Christ Church. It is still standing, attached to the Synod Hall of the cathedral.

If the street pattern in this area remained much the same from pre-Norman times, the actual appearance of the streets would have changed considerably. The old Viking houses of the tenth and eleventh centuries were one-storey post-and-wattle jobs, placed closely together, and with a likely life of only twenty or thirty years. By the early thirteenth century, after three decades of Norman Bristol rule, these houses would have been largely going out of fashion. The exodus of many of the old Hiberno-Norse families, ousted across the bridge to Oxmantown on the northern bank of the Liffey, meant that there was probably a considerable change in the make-up of the city's population, with many having coming across the Irish Sea from the west of England and beyond to seek greater fortune in Bristol's new acquisition. With them, they would have brought their Romanesque and Gothic church-building styles, but also a different type of house, of the kind that they would have been accustomed to at home. These were two-storey, half-timbered dwellings with pointed roofs and gables facing onto the street. The same materials may have been used in the single-storey storage sheds, where merchandise unloaded at the quayside would have been kept.

What cannot be read from a picture like this is the smell that must have pervaded the streets of Dublin throughout the medieval period, arising from offal dumped in the streets and the lack of sewage systems which could have made life more pleasant. Some ladies may have been rich

IMPORT/EXPORT

At the foot of Winetavern Street we see the Wood Quay area just before the final medieval extension, when a stone quay-front was added. Various reclamations have resulted in rows of warehouses and other stores. Boats that are descendants of the flat-bottomed Viking vessels are tied up beside the wooden quay, where goods can be weighed using the crane in the centre of the picture. Cargo such as wine and timber is seen waiting for distribution, while some livestock are going for export. Much larger boats wait out in Dublin Bay, as they are too heavy to come to the quays – they are serviced by smaller vessels.

enough to have perfume to offset the odorous stench.

The most noticeable development in the city's appearance that can be credited to the Normans was the filling-in of the area between the old town wall of *c.*1100 and the river-front. This may partially be explained by the size of boats. Before the coming of the Normans, most boats would have had to have been small to unload their cargoes on the mud-flats at the river's edge. The tradition of the old Viking ships with one mast and a single sail would seem to have continued into the Norman period, unlike in the North Sea and the Baltic, where the cogs and hulks of the Hanseatic League were developed to carry more and heavier cargo. Strakes — timbers used in building the sides of boats, of which a number were found as waste infill during the 1970s excavations in Wood Quay — showed that as and from the year 1200, the size of boats had grown in comparison to those of the previous century. But that very size created problems in unloading these vessels, so improved methods of docking were needed in order to accommodate these larger vessels — which is what brought about the great changes in Wood Quay. The edge of the river kept on being pushed back further and further northwards, so that by the thirteenth century the area between the old city wall and the present Quays had been largely infilled. A new stone quay was constructed around 1260, which kept the river at bay but also allowed larger boats to come directly to the quayside to discharge their cargo. The name 'Wood Quay' may have come about because of timber imported here for houses and other things.

An important part of the ships' cargo was wine, which came from the Bordeaux region of western France to still the thirst of Dubliners; they had cultivated this taste before the Normans ever came. It is no coincidence that the main street leading from the quayside to the area around Christ Church and Dublin Castle (seen in the top left of the main image) was called Winetavern Street, and it boasted of having the city's Guild Hall halfway up its hill. The wine was imported in pottery vessels of so-called Saintonge ware, but the Dublin excavations also uncovered great numbers of broken potsherds which had come from Ham Green near Bristol. Dublin, too, had its potters producing a variety of vessels, from the simple to the decorative. Other imports would have included luxury items for the richer echelons, but also some of the simpler necessities of life such as salt.

The boats moored at Wood Quay that brought in these items would also have served the export trade. Raw materials from the hinterland, but also from Gaelic Ireland, would have been channelled through Dublin to be sent abroad, and that included a great amount of fish. In the late Middle Ages, wool became an extremely important staple of the export trade, and hides were traded as far

away as Italy for the leather industry, doubtless encouraged by Italian bankers operating in Ireland particularly in the thirteenth century. During that period and well into the following century, Dublin flourished as a port, but the Black Death of 1348–1350 had a disastrous effect on the city's economy.

Worse was to come for Wood Quay two and a half centuries later. The most vital machinery for loading and unloading ships were the cranes, two of which are seen here along the quay. In 1597 they were being used to carry ashore gunpowder in barrels that had been transferred from larger ships moored in Dublin Bay onto smaller lighters, which could defy the silt of the River Liffey to reach as far as Wood Quay. The gunpowder was intended for use by the English commanders in Dublin Castle against Hugh O'Neill in the Nine Years' War. As it was being unloaded, a spark was set off (no one knows how), unleashing a vast explosion that left well over a hundred people dead and destroyed many of the houses within a radius of a few hundred yards.

An explosion of a very different kind was to drag Wood Quay into the limelight again almost four centuries later. Dublin Corporation wanted to build extensive city offices on the site. In 1969, the National Museum, which had been conducting excavations around Christ Church since the early 1960s, moved into an area that would not have been affected by the office buildings and began to expose many metres of Viking material below the surface, including the well-preserved lower parts of wattle houses. When planning permission was granted for the Civic Offices in 1972, public disquiet became palpable about what unique and invaluable archaeological material might be lost forever as a result of digging the foundations for these buildings. Sadly, the National Museum did not resist the plans, though it continued digging for a further four years.

By the beginning of 1978, the imminence of destruction led to a court case that declared the site to be a National Monument in the care of the State. Within days, Dublin Corporation sought the consent of the Office of Public Works (whose duty it was to protect National Monuments) to negate the ruling. Incensed, the public reacted furiously and held a meeting in the Lord Mayor's Mansion House early in September 1978. A few weeks later, around twenty thousand people (of whom the author was one) marched to the site to protest against the Corporation's callous indifference to Ireland's archaeological heritage. Archaeologists stood up to the bulldozers and were joined by others in occupying the site, yet they were powerless in the face of a legal agreement between the Corporation and the OPW that had been signed months before, taking advantage of a loophole in the National Monuments Act. Not even the government of the day knew about the agreement, and despite appeals from Nordic and other international bodies to find a sensible solution – and despite a further legal injunction, which the Corporation got the Supreme Court to overrule – the buildings went ahead, destroying much that would have shed further light on early Dubliners. An important casualty was the stone wall of c.1100, which flashes across the centre of the picture here. It was almost entirely demolished and, despite promises, never rebuilt, though a part of it is actually preserved in the basement of the Civic Offices.

The whole Wood Quay saga of the 1970s is not an edifying story about those who promoted and acquiesced in the building of the Civic Offices, but an heroic one for those who fought to preserve as much of Viking and medieval Dublin as possible. If it all had one benefit, it was that the people of Ireland changed their views of the Vikings from being the monk-bashers of the early Irish Annals to being the 'good guys' who started our cities and our coinage, and who taught the Irish how to build the boats that enabled us to expand our horizons.

AN ANGLO-NORMAN WOMAN

The woman is dressed lightly for summer in a linen kirtle, a type of garment that was in use for several centuries. Her red leather purse hangs to one side. She lives inside the town walls and has bought some green-leafed plants and beans for cooking. Excavations in Dublin revealed much about how such Dubliners lived and cooked. In the early medieval period, the main material for utensils was wood, but after an increase in trade with Bristol and beyond, pottery — both imported and home-produced — became the norm. Jugs, cooking pots and jars were in use, as were iron knives and spoons made of wood or bone.

MEDI

RELIC

L   I

ST. MARY'S ABBEY

W hen considering medieval Dublin, most people think of the city south of the Liffey – the castle, the two cathedrals and the numerous houses nestling beneath their respective walls, not to mention the excavations some decades ago which brought so much of Viking Dublin to light. But, as Professor Howard Clarke constantly reminds us, there were also suburbs stretching in all four cardinal directions from the city centre.

One of those north of the Liffey is Oxmantown, a name derived from Ostman-town, the home of the Ostmen, that is, the Vikings. At the height of Viking Dublin in the tenth century, there was probably little more than green fields there, though the possibility cannot be discounted that there was a Celtic church on the site of St. Michan's (on today's Church Street), which is the small church with the tall tower in the main picture, on the far side of the settlement. It is not too far away from the original river crossing at the 'Ford of the hurdle-work' (*Áth Cliath*, the Irish name for Dublin). This may have provided access to and from the Slige Midluachra, the main road from Ulster, which terminated at the Liffey, where it would have joined up with two other major early Irish roads coming from Connacht and south Leinster respectively.

The bridge erected by the Irish High King Maelsechlainn II in 1001 (the predecessor of today's Fr. Mathew Bridge) would have been marginally downstream from the ford, and would have provided an impetus for the population to expand to the north side of the Liffey, facilitated by the extension of the town walls westwards to allow guarded access to the bridge. Described as 'Dubhgall's Bridge' in the early twelfth century, this could indicate that it was called after a man of that name, which means 'black foreigner', or that it was seen as the 'bridge of the black foreigners', usually meaning Danish rather than Norwegian Vikings. One way or another, that bridge may have been responsible for opening up the northern suburb on the opposite side of the river. It would certainly seem to have given the Hiberno-Norse population of Dublin an opportunity to escape the domination of the Normans when they arrived in the city in 1171, and their settlement in Ostmantown would probably have followed shortly after that.

There was a gate at the northern end of the bridge called 'Ostmans' Gate' (no longer extant), which would have led to the present Church Street. There was, however, one major structure that was erected in Ostmantown before the Hiberno-Norse inhabitants had crossed the bridge to live there after the arrival of the Normans, and that was St. Mary's Abbey, which fills out much of the right-hand side of the main picture and the inset below. One of the first

THE PLAN OF ST. MARY'S ABBEY

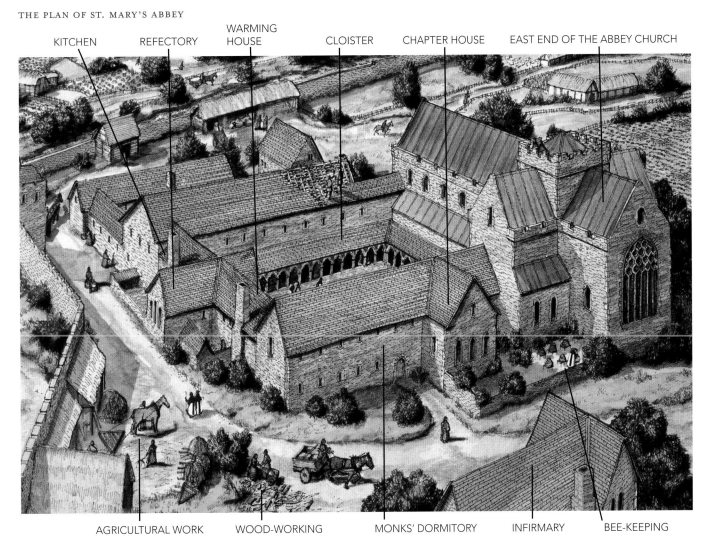

KITCHEN   REFECTORY   WARMING HOUSE   CLOISTER   CHAPTER HOUSE   EAST END OF THE ABBEY CHURCH

AGRICULTURAL WORK   WOOD-WORKING   MONKS' DORMITORY   INFIRMARY   BEE-KEEPING

monasteries to be founded as part of the religious reform movement initiated by St. Malachy of Armagh, it started out as a reformed Benedictine daughter-house of Savigny in France in 1139, but when all the other houses of the same order joined the Cistercians in 1147/1148, St. Mary's followed suit.

The Cistercians lived according to the rule of St. Benedict. Like the Savigny monks, the order began in France at the great abbey of Cîteaux, where the famous preacher St. Bernard started his monastic life. It was in his arms that St. Malachy died in 1148 at the monastery of Clairvaux. The Cistercians are credited with the introduction of proper farming in Ireland. Their houses were usually out in the countryside and often beside a stream, as was the case with the first Irish Cistercian monastery at Mellifont in County Louth. St. Mary's was beside the River Bradoge, closer to a town than most other Cistercian houses in Ireland. Precisely why the site at the present Meetinghouse Lane off Capel Street was chosen no one knows, but perhaps its proximity to businesses along the Liffey may have played a role.

Today, only the chapter house of St. Mary's remains, a Gothic vaulted structure well below the current ground level outside. In medieval times, it was an important meeting place for official functions. It was here that Silken Thomas FitzGerald famously and impetuously threw down the Sword of State in a rebellious act against the English King Henry VIII in 1534 as part of a campaign to conquer Dublin Castle; this act of treason led to his beheading in an English prison three years later. The abbots of the monastery were often government officials, and through bequests and donations, as well as what it received from oft-disputed fishing rights, St. Mary's became in time one of the three richest Cistercian foundations in Britain or Ireland. Its wealth enabled it to produce manuscripts now preserved in London, Oxford, Cambridge and Manchester. One of the most important of these, dating from the fourteenth century, was acquired by the Library of Trinity College, Dublin, in 2014.

In *Ulysses*, James Joyce may have been a little wide of the mark in describing the chapter house of St. Mary's as 'the most historic spot in all Dublin', but in its heyday, the monastery must have been a highly impressive building close to the Liffey. It played host to many important visitors and was also very generous in feeding the poor, who must have greatly missed it when Henry VIII suppressed the monastery in 1539. The buildings survived above ground until late in the following century, when their stones were used in building Essex (now Grattan) Bridge further down the Liffey. Some fine fragments of cloister discovered in 1975 in Cook Street on the south side of the Liffey were

very probably removed from St. Mary's at about this time and used as building rubble.

Various excavations have taken place over the last century and a quarter to see if any of the foundations of this important abbey were still to be found below ground, but sadly without any great success. Because St. Mary's was a Savigny foundation, which was close to the Cistercians, it is quite likely that its design would generally have followed the normal plan of a Cistercian monastery, which – with minor adjustments in scale – was fairly standard throughout the whole of Europe, and which is seen in the accompanying illustration. The scheme would have had a long church, with nave, aisle, transepts and a squat,

THE ROAD FROM THE NORTH

Near St. Mary's were two other religious institutions: in the centre-right of this detail is St. Michan's, on what may have been the site of a Celtic church; on the left is St. Saviour's Dominican Priory, shown here after its second rebuilding following Edward Bruce's invasion of 1315. The road running between the two towers leads off to the left to the site of the modern Fr. Mathew Bridge. It was part of the most important route to Dublin from the north. The houses are typical of this period; one famous example, on the corner of Werburgh Street and Castle Street, survived into the nineteenth century.

square tower, standing at one side of an open-air cloister garth; a sacristy and chapter house (the only part of St. Mary's to survive, along with a covered way called a 'slype' giving access to the outside world) on another; a refectory and a kitchen on the side opposite the church; and store-rooms and first-floor sleeping accommodation on the fourth side. The artist has based the whole complex on similar Irish Cistercian houses such as Jerpoint, County Kilkenny, and Holy Cross, County Tipperary, with the addition here of a stout wall surrounding the monastery which is mentioned in historical records, and which probably had a towered entrance gateway.

With the exception of the Savigny monks and their even earlier foundation at Erenagh in County Down, the Cistercians were the first major monastic order to come to Ireland as part of St. Malachy's scheme to reform the church in Ireland during the first half of the twelfth century. They were followed in 1224 by the Dominicans, whose first foundation in Ireland was just down the road from St. Mary's, between what are now the Four Courts

and Church Street, on a site presented to them by the monks of St. Mary's and seen on the extreme left of the main picture. Known as St. Saviour's, it was completed in 1228 but burned down in a disastrous fire in 1304 that also affected St. Mary's. Afterwards, it was ordered to be rebuilt — but worse was yet to come. When Edward Bruce, brother of Robert, King of Scotland, invaded Ireland in 1315 and threatened to occupy the city of Dublin, the Dominican church had many of its stones removed to strengthen the city walls and two gates on the opposite side of the river. Afterwards it was rebuilt and lasted until it, too, was suppressed in 1539. The site was later taken over by lawyers for use as the King's Inns before they moved to their present site on Constitution Hill (see p. 134).

By the Later Middle Ages, private houses had begun to spread north of the Liffey in Ostmantown. None of these survived, but they were doubtless half-timbered structures, as seen along the streets in this bird's eye view from above what is now Capel Street.

BUSINESS ABROAD

St. Mary's Abbey was well placed to trade goods with Dublin, just across the Liffey, or to export them further afield. Older maps of Dublin show boats of smaller draft tied up along the quays, while larger vessels would have anchored in the bay. The type of boat shown here is called a cog, and it was used for trade in the waters all round Europe and beyond. Cogs were much favoured by the traders of the Hanseatic League.

A CISTERCIAN MONK

The monks of St. Mary's Abbey conformed to the rule of St. Benedict. Their day was structured around the service of **matins,** beginning at midnight, followed by the morning office of **lauds** at 3am. Afterwards they would retire for a few hours of sleep and then rise at 6am to wash and attend the office of **prime.** They then gathered in the chapter house to receive instructions for the day. Then came either private mass, spiritual reading or work until 9am, when the office of **terce** was said, followed by high mass. At noon came the office of **sext** and the midday meal. After a brief period of communal recreation, the monks rested until the office of **none** at 3pm. Then farming and housekeeping followed until after twilight, the evening prayer of **vespers** at 6pm, the night prayer of **compline** at 9pm, and off to bed until the cycle began again.

This monk is a scribe, and he holds a trimmed quill in his left hand. Hanging from his belt on the left of the picture is a small penner for holding quills, and next to it hangs a small inkwell (also called an inkhorn). On his left hangs a hollowed-out horn, which is used for other colours and clipped to his belt when empty.

St. Patrick's Cathedral is best known in many circles through its most famous dean, Jonathan Swift, the author of *Gulliver's Travels*, whose idea of untrammelled, outspoken criticism independent of any church authority continues among his successors. The cathedral is also well known in Dublin as the venue for wonderful Christmas carol singing. Its history goes way back before Swift's time (he was dean from 1713 until his death in 1745), though its links with Ireland's patron saint date from hundreds of years after Patrick's death in the fifth century. The old tradition that St. Patrick baptised people here should be taken with grains of salt and discarded along with his banishment of snakes — which were not there for him to banish! The present cathedral does preserve some cross-decorated grave monuments dating back to the eleventh or twelfth century, which are our first witnesses to Christianity on the site.

An earlier church dedicated to St. Patrick is reported to have stood on an island in the River Poddle, the course of which was moved slightly to the west to allow for the building to be kept on dry land. In due course, this pre-cathedral church was raised in status by being given a number of priests who were supported by monies coming from various churches, almost all located outside the city. But the Archbishop of Dublin, Henry Blund of London — whose portrait appears on the Waterford Royal Charter — decided that its status should be raised further by making it into a cathedral, and this necessitated the creation of a new and larger structure. Preachers were sent around the country to gather money for the build, and they had not completed their task before the archbishop died in 1228. Building, however, went ahead, and the cathedral was completed for dedication on St. Patrick's Day in 1254 — probably much faster than similar structures in most of Europe's capital cities. It was, nevertheless, more low-lying than Christ Church, which led to occasional flooding during the Later Middle Ages, doubtless causing damage to some of the cathedral's archives.

To both the Irish and outsiders, Dublin seems to be unique in having two cathedrals (both now Protestant) within only five hundred metres of each other. Christ Church is the older of the two; St. Laurence O'Toole, the twelfth-century Archbishop of Dublin who died in 1180, made it into a monastic establishment of the Arroasian Canons of St. Augustine, who had been introduced from France. In contrast, St. Patrick's was a purely secular cathedral whose function was more administrative within the diocese of Dublin. Their respective roles did not gen-

erally clash, which helps to explain why there are two cathedrals: Christ Church within the city walls and St. Patrick's without. Nevertheless, their proximity did occasionally lead to disputes about elections, and about who should precede whom in ceremonial processions. By the time of the Reformation, Queen Elizabeth I's Lord Deputy, Sir John Perrot, was able to comment that this little city 'has two great cathedral churches, richly endowed and too near together for any good they do'! In 1872, St. Patrick's became the national cathedral of all the Church of Ireland, and Christ Church became the cathedral of Dublin alone.

MINOT'S TOWER

Thomas Minot, Archbishop of Dublin, commissioned this imposing forty-five-metre-high tower at the north-west angle of St. Patrick's Cathedral in the 1360s. It is still known as Minot's Tower, although what we see today dates from a rebuilding at the end of the fourteenth century. The tower now houses a peal of bells – donated by Edward Cecil Guinness in 1897 – on the fourth floor, two storeys above the ringing chamber. The granite spire, over thirty metres high, was designed by George Semple and added to the top of the tower in the mid-eighteenth century. To the right of the tower, we can see a bridge over the River Poddle.

ST. SEPULCHRE'S PALACE

St Sepulchre's, the palace of the medieval archbishops of Dublin, is located to the east of St. Patrick's Cathedral. It was named in commemoration of the crusade to recapture the Church of the Holy Sepulchre in Jerusalem and included a medieval court for trying most crimes. It remained the seat of the archbishops of Dublin until 1806, after which it became a State courthouse and police station. Today it gives a sense of antiquity from the impressive early seventeenth-century gateway to the castellated double front, but it has lost its integrity. After almost a century as a Garda barracks, this complex could find another use as a museum.

St. Patrick's Cathedral is one of the longest (if not the longest) and also one of the finest to have been built in medieval Ireland, its scale and beauty being Ireland's best comparison to the grandiose Gothic examples in Britain and on the Continent. Given the fact that its designers and builders were English prelates, it is no surprise that it has been compared to Salisbury Cathedral, though its plan is closer to Salisbury's predecessor nearby at Old Sarum. Dublin's denizens must have stood in wonderment as the seventeen-metre-high building proceeded, and its mas-

termind, Archbishop Henry Blund, must have been very happy with his new creation, though he didn't live to see its completion. That pleasure fell to his successor, Luke, in 1254.

In comparison to the more old-fashioned Romanesque style of the choir and transepts of Christ Church, on which building started around 1180, St. Patrick's was all in the latest English architectural style, making it the finest and most refined Gothic church in Ireland (even if its present interior owes much to nineteenth-century restoration). Henry Blund, however, put his own particular stamp on the design by providing both transepts with their own east and west arcades. At the extreme eastern end, behind the high altar, was a 'lady chapel' dedicated to the Virgin Mary. It was built by Archbishop Fulk de Saundford, the first Dublin archbishop to be buried in St. Patrick's rather than Christ Church, as had been the case heretofore. An unusual feature is the square tower outside the north-western corner of the nave, whose orientation differs curiously from the remainder of the cathedral. Originally built by Archbishop Thomas Minot, it must have at least partially fallen victim to a fire in the cathedral in 1362. Shortly afterwards, Minot got 'sixty straggling and idle fellows' to rebuild the steeple. He may have regretted that decision, as the tower collapsed again in 1394, and it owes its present form to a rebuild around the year 1400. The existing spire was not added until 1750.

St. Patrick's Cathedral certainly made its presence felt on the Dublin skyline, with walls rising higher than any other structure in the city, and it also made itself heard, both literally and metaphorically. Its peal of bells has tolled since medieval times, ringing out on important occasions and feast days. It would also have been heard during processions that took place outside the building, particularly on Palm Sunday, when participants would stop at 'stations' to say prescribed prayers. Other important processions took place, naturally, on St. Patrick's Day and on the feast of Corpus Christi. But it was within the walls that most of the ecclesiastical liturgy would have been practised. An essential part of that was music. Originally this was exclusively plain chant, but polyphony would have become more common during the fourteenth century. A choir school was opened in 1432 and, as Ireland's oldest, it continues to this day to provide choristers for the singing of sacred music in the cathedral. We are fortunate that one thirteenth-century manuscript (now in Cambridge) survives to give us details of what would have been sung. Just as the plan of St. Patrick's was based on that of the Old Sarum Cathedral near Salisbury, so also was its liturgy. Architecture and liturgy combined in the lady chapel at the eastern end of the cathedral, built during the thirteenth century as an addition at the back of the choir to facilitate liturgy devoted to honouring the 'Lady', the Virgin Mary, mother of Christ. Following extensive restoration work, the lady chapel was opened to the public in 2013.

Only yards away from St. Patrick's Cathedral, to the east, was St. Sepulchre's, the palace of the medieval archbishops of Dublin (now home to Kevin Street Garda Station!). The nearness of the two worked, on the whole, to the cathedral's advantage, though the odd flare-up did occur over elections, and particularly over who was to make decisions until the candidate for office was finally chosen. Significantly, both the palace and the cathedral were outside the city walls, resulting in St. Patrick's having less to do with the civic authorities and the city than with the colonial administrators in Dublin Castle, where knowledge of canon law among St. Patrick's secular clerks proved to be useful.

By the sixteenth century, St. Patrick's had a much richer cathedral chapter than that of Christ Church, not arising from direct offerings from the faithful but from the contributions of churches that the cathedral owned well outside the city boundary. Its dignitaries and canons were allowed to engage in non-religious activities that earned them extra money, leaving the poor vicars choral and minor canons to get on with the real job of providing divine service throughout the week. But it was this very wealth that attracted Henry VIII's Royal Commissioners, who dissolved St. Patrick's Cathedral in 1547 with a view to purloining its valuables. The buildings in the cathedral grounds known as 'the Liberties' were given over to administrative uses, law courts and a store for records. Within a decade, St. Patrick's re-opened for Catholic worship under Queen Mary I, but it was under her successor, Elizabeth I, that the cathedral first changed over to its present Protestant status; not, however, for divine worship, but for preaching and lectures.

The cathedral was once more dissolved under the Puritan Oliver Cromwell. It re-opened again after Charles II came to the throne in 1660, after which its land and property were duly restored, the dispersed chapter re-assembled, and a dozen new bishops consecrated. Under his son and successor, James II, many feared that the cathedral would become Catholic again, but his defeats at Derry, Aughrim and the Boyne in 1689–1691 gave St. Patrick's the opportunity of celebrating the victory of his Protestant opponent, William of Orange.

Under Jonathan Swift's deanship in the first half of the eighteenth century, an intellectual life developed in the cathedral, and the Protestant working class living in the neighbourhood applauded Swift for his outspoken remarks about England's interference in Ireland's affairs. By the nineteenth century, parts of the cathedral were in danger of collapse, but through a generous injection of money by Sir Benjamin Lee Guinness of the famous brewing family, St. Patrick's was restored to its present glory, with only minor interventions in the years since. Thus both Dublin cathedrals owe their preservation to the thirst of the nation, as it was the whiskey distiller Henry Roe who supplied the wherewithal to restore Christ Church Cathedral at about the same time.

A CANON OF
ST. PATRICK'S CATHEDRAL

There is some visual reference for the clergy of St. Patrick's in the form of a stone effigy of Archbishop Fulk de Saundford (in office 1256–1271), which can be seen in the cathedral's north choir aisle, but here we are looking at a canon. He appears to be praying, and he is wearing a purple maniple on his left arm, indicating that he is on his way to a Mass. For much of his day, he would be thinking about the law relating to the properties of the cathedral. The chapter included people who specialised in the administration of the church and diocese, and who were in communication with the authorities nearby in Dublin Castle.

The canon does not belong to a monastic order. He wears a white linen alb, tied around the middle with a cincture. His outer vestment, the purple chasuble, is folded up at the front, as he will perform the role of deacon in the Mass that is about to take place.

CEN
OF PO

DUBLIN CASTLE

circa 1475

A s can be seen in an earlier picture of Norman Dublin as it was around 1275 (see pp. 30–31), the castle was perched on a prominent ridge at the south-eastern corner of the town defences, which emanated from it. But this was not the earliest fortification on the site. Excavations in 1985–1987 in the Powder Tower on the extreme left of the illustration on the previous pages showed that when its lowermost portions were being built by the Normans, an earlier Viking wall was found to be extant, though not to any great height. It consisted of a series of earthen banks, one of which was provided with a stone facing to prevent erosion from the River Poddle, which lapped up against it, having already passed through *Dubh Linn*, the Black Pool, just above it.

The historical castle was not begun until 1204 – but that is more than thirty years after King Henry II took over Dublin and gave it to his 'favourite men of Bristol'. It is unlikely that the newly arrived Normans would have left the town defenceless for these three decades. In many other parts of the country, the Normans built 'mottes' – round-shaped, flat-topped earthen mounds with a wooden tower on top – from which to survey the surrounding countryside for any potential aggressors as they stood to control the land they had recently won from the native Irish. If, as is possible, a motte had been erected in the area of Dublin Castle, not a trace of it survives; even if it had existed, it would almost certainly have been demolished when plans were afoot to build the new stone fortification in 1204.

This came about through an edict of King John (he who was forced to issue the

The main gate into Dublin Castle is shown here with a barbican in front. While there is so far no archaeological evidence of the barbican, such a free-standing structure would have provided an extra defence for the main castle, being linked to the main gate by a second short bridge not visible from this angle. The main gate, known from depictions from the late Tudor period, leads into the medieval Great Courtyard, today the Upper Castle Yard enclosure.

famous *Magna Carta* eleven years later), who had visited Ireland in 1185, eight years after being granted the Lordship of Ireland by his father, Henry II. His mandate of 1204 was issued to his illegitimate brother, Meiler FitzHenry, and ran as follows:

You have intimated to us that you have no place about you where our treasure can be stored; and, in as much for that purpose as well as for many other, a fortalice may be necessary for us at Dublin, we give you mandate to have a castle made there in a suitable place where you shall see best so as to curb and, if need be, to defend the city, making it as strong as you can with good ditches and strong walls. And you shall first make a tower where at a later time the castle and bailey and other requirements may be suitably made, provided we shall give you a mandate for that.

Being interested in money and taxation, King John made sure that he wasn't going to pay for the castle directly himself, but ordered Meiler to get the building costs from one 'G. FitzRobert' who owed him money – a clever way of getting a return on his loan.

For reasons of stability, the castle would have been essentially made of stone. Construction started around 1210 and was completed two decades or more later. We know that timber was brought from Wicklow in 1213 to help in the building. Surprisingly, perhaps, custody of the castle was given to the Archbishop of Dublin, Henry Blund of London, who had to be compensated for losses sustained during the construction work. He may not have been the best adviser, as the structure needed extensive

THE CASTLE TOWERS AND BEYOND

Two towers of the castle are visible here. The nearer one is the Store-house or Powder Tower, whose surroundings were excavated in the 1980s, revealing some Viking and Hiberno-Norse remains. The more distant one is the Record Tower, formerly the Black Tower – the only intact medieval tower in the castle today. Outside, between the two is visible the marshy ground where once the dark pool, *Dubh Linn*, was fed by the River Poddle. In the upper left, in the distance, is a suggestion of St. Stephen's Church and leper hospital, from which St. Stephen's Green takes its name. To the left of the Record Tower is visible St. Peter's Church, shown roofless; near the top right, St. Mary's Priory boasts a tower.

repairs only five years or so after completion and again in 1250. By 1265 it had to be re-fortified, and early in the following century, repairs had to be undertaken to the justiciar's chambers and some of the towers, as well as to the stables.

By that time, the central court of the castle had had one major addition to it, the King's Hall (seen on the right of the main picture, with the five large windows). Measuring over thirty-six metres long and half of that in width, it was ordered to be built by King Henry III in 1243 'after the manner of the hall at Canterbury', with a large, round window in the gable and a painting of the king and queen within. Work was interrupted the following year but continued in 1245, when the order was made that it be supplied with water from the town aqueduct. As with the castle walls that surrounded it, repairs and renewals were often

required down the years; the hall at one stage served as a weapons store and was recorded in 1584 as being 'still ruinous owing to a gunpowder explosion'. The building lasted for just another century, as it was burned down in a major fire in 1684.

The following century and a half saw the rise of what is now known as the Upper Castle Yard. It is indeed surprising that so little remains of the stout medieval castle. The most significant remnant is the Record Tower, seen in the upper left of the main illustration, which links the Lower and Upper Castle Yard and adjoins the early-nineteenth-century Chapel Royal (at that time, the tower's battlements were also added). Its security cannot have been great, as one – in fact two – famous prisoner escapes probably took place from the Record Tower. In 1587, the young and romantic Red Hugh O'Donnell was lured aboard a ship at Rathmullan in his native Donegal under the pretence of getting him to sample wine, whereupon he was seized by the queen's viceroy and brought as a prisoner to Dublin Castle. Three years later he escaped but was hastily recaptured. However, the following year, he tried again and managed to get away through the December rain and snow of the Dublin and Wicklow mountains, a swashbuckling feat that inspired the 1966 Disney film *The Fighting Prince of Donegal*. O'Donnell was subsequently defeated at the Battle of Kinsale in 1601, and he fled to Spain, where he died. The terrifying regime from which he had escaped is illustrated in the earliest picture we have of Dublin Castle, printed in John Derricke's *The Image of Irelande* (1581). It shows the viceroy, Sir Henry Sidney, riding out through the main gate of the castle (seen in the detail on p. 69), which is flanked by a tower on each side.

KEY TO THE CASTLE

CHURCH OF ST. MICHAEL-LE-POLE AND ITS GAELIC ROUND TOWER

PALACE OF ST. SEPULCHRE

THE SQUARE TOWER, LATER REDUCED IN HEIGHT TO FORM A GUN PLATFORM

ST. PATRICK'S CATHEDRAL

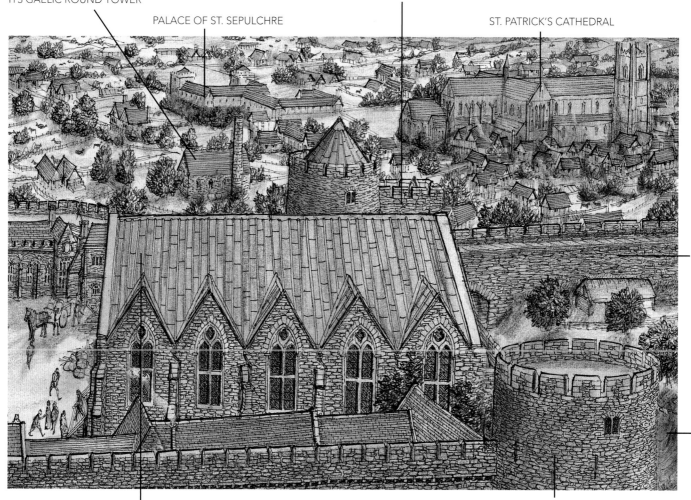

THE TOWN WALL

WESTERN SIDE OF THE MOAT

THE GREAT HALL, ORDERED BY KING HENRY III IN 1243

THE CORKE TOWER, THE REMAINS OF WHICH SUPPORT THE MODERN INTERNATIONAL CONFERENCE CENTRE

Above the portcullis are the decapitated heads of bearded Irishmen put to death by Elizabeth I's forces – a reminder of what would happen to those who did not obey her stern orders.

The castle itself had a lucky escape when, during the fierce winter of 1317, Dublin was in danger of being captured by the Scottish invader Edward Bruce, who was crowned King of Ireland in 1315 and threatened to march on the city. The mayor at the time burned some of the town's western suburbs to ensure that they would not be taken. He took stones from St. Mary del Dam and other churches to boost the fortifications, and also blocked up one of the gates to prevent Bruce entering the precincts. Like Napoleon centuries later, Bruce never arrived in Dublin, and St. Mary del Dam was restored shortly afterwards. But the real disaster was to occur in the middle of the same century.

The Black Death, a plague that ravaged Europe during the years 1348–1350, was introduced into Ireland by boats mooring in the port of Howth, eight miles from Dublin Castle. It spread rapidly, and its effects were quickly felt throughout the country, particularly in towns, where the population lived cheek by jowl in confined spaces in which contamination could easily occur. Whatever the population of Dublin was at the time, the Black Death probably reduced it by at least 40 per cent in three years. It took the city many years to get back on its feet again, whereas in the less affected rural areas of the country, plenty of church-building went on, in comparison to the paucity of similar construction in the country's capital.

The Dublin Castle we see today is a far cry from the fortress illustrated here as it was in the later fifteenth century. The Record Tower and part of the Bermingham Tower are virtually all that remain to remind today's visitor of the strength of the castle in the medieval period. The Upper Castle Yard, where the medieval castle stood, is now a quiet place for conferences and great ceremonial events, most notably the inauguration of the Republic's presidents in the State Apartments' St. Patrick's Hall. It was in the Upper Yard, too, that the British government handed over Dublin Castle to Michael Collins and others representing the fledgling Irish State in 1922, after seven hundred years of English rule.

A GUARD OF
DUBLIN CASTLE

This is not a popular subject, as the Dublin Castle guards came to symbolise English rule in Ireland. In reality, it must have been a mixed body of men over the centuries; first a Norman defence force to keep the Pale surrounding Dublin intact, and later, part of a Tudor army that suppressed the native Irish population with great severity.

In this picture we see a fighting man of the late fifteenth century. His weapon is the crossbow, capable of inflicting terrible wounds. He wears a gambeson, a padded jacket that contains many layers of fabric to provide extra protection, over the top of his chain mail. A gambeson could have removable sleeves, as is the case here.

On January 16th, 1922, Michael Collins arrived in Dublin Castle to receive the handover of the Castle on behalf of the new Irish Free State government. Lord Lieutenant FitzAlan — with a surname as Norman as any commander of the castle guard in 1204 — is reported to have commented, 'You are seven minutes late, Mr. Collins.' To which he received the reply, 'We've been waiting over seven hundred years. You can have the extra seven minutes.'

THE TAILORS' HALL

Other than the cathedrals, churches and the walls of Dublin City and Castle, some of the most persistent survivors of the medieval period in the burgeoning capital of the eighteenth century were the guilds. They were responsible for the organisation of trades and industries; they maintained the quality of their crafts and exercised a strict monopoly on membership. The various guilds had a history going back to the thirteenth century, with the general merchants (such as the Guild of the Holy Trinity) being among the most influential. But there were scores of others, with the goldsmiths at the top of the pile, followed (in no particular order) by feltmakers, plasterers and bricklayers, coopers, brewers and others. Compared to modern trade unions, they were valuable employers who helped keep trade going.

One of the most significant was the Tailors' Guild or Corporation of Tailors. It played a political role by helping financially to keep the old medieval city walls repaired, and also extended its influence farther out beyond the Pale, that movable defence designed to protect the capital from intruders. The tailors were also sufficiently in funds to be able to make a loan to none other than the Lord Lieutenant, the English king's representative in Ireland, and when it came to their place in the imposing processions that took place in the city, they were second only to the merchants' Holy Trinity Guild. These processions were an annual affair and would have competed in size with the modern St. Patrick's Day parade. The tailors usually borrowed the best horses from their gentleman clients and paraded for hours around the city, joining others

PLOTTING REVOLUTION

The scene here is set in 1790s, when the Tailors' Hall was being used by the 'Back Lane Parliament' (see p.78) and the United Irishmen. Theobald Wolfe Tone was working on his campaign to extend greater rights to the whole population. Such meetings in the Tailors' Hall must have involved considerable tension, given the building's proximity to Dublin Castle, just a short distance away. The figure approaching in the bottom right has passed through the impressive gateway that still stands on Back Lane; it is now free-standing, where once it was surrounding by buildings.

who had a very large coach with a platform and canopy, a predecessor of the modern float. These processions usually took place on the Feast of St. John the Baptist in high summer, and they were followed by a picnic, with plays being performed in the old medieval tradition.

The tailors had organised themselves sufficiently well in the sixteenth century that they were able to build themselves a hall, which not many of the other guilds would have had. This probably had a wooden framework, with stone additions. Though we hear of the tailors ensconcing themselves in the newly constructed guild hall in the Tholsel in 1683 – a place fairly central in the old part of the city between Christ Church and St. Patrick's Cathedral – their original hall was in Back Lane, a small thoroughfare just inside the old city wall, and it seems to have continued in

use until it was replaced on the same site by the present Tailors' Hall. What its builders probably did not realise was that beneath them lay metres of Viking Dublin, and just how deep these layers were became clear when excavations were carried out along High Street, at the back of the hall, in the 1960s.

The location was very close to Christ Church and only a few hundred yards from Dublin Castle, which enabled the tailors on occasion to show their loyalty to the English crown. Their patron saint was John the Baptist, in whose church on Fishamble Street, not far away, they had pews. But after the short-lived reign of King James II in the city, life became very difficult for Catholics both inside and outside the Guild. Protestants dominated every aspect of the organisation's activities, their numbers swelled by the arrival of Huguenot craftsmen after 1691.

During the years on either side of 1700, the English were getting worried about the success of woollen exports from Ireland, as it was damaging their trade to the new colonies in North America — to such an extent that the English banned Irish exports in 1699. The tailors may have profited from this, as there would have been more raw material available from which to make their clients' clothes. It certainly appears that they had money, since they started to build their new hall on the site of the old one only four years later.

The present Tailors' Hall, the only surviving guild hall in Dublin, was started in 1703 and completed four years later under the supervision of one Mr. Richard Mills, assistant to the Master of the City Works, who may also have been the architect. Its access is through a contemporary gateway, which was flanked by shops and houses up to a century ago. Inside, the main room is on the left, lit by remarkably high windows. This is a tall hall, 13.7 metres long and almost half of that in height. It would have had a minstrels' gallery at one end, and at the other end a throne for the Master, surmounted by the Guild's crest, which no longer survives. A fine chimney piece was added in 1784; later stolen, it was subsequently restored. Beneath the hall

NEIGHBOURING TOWERS

On the right here, we see Christ Church Cathedral at a low point in its history. It would be almost another century before George Edmund Street – with financial help from distiller Henry Roe – would undertake his extensive renovations. To its left is the tower of St. Michael's Church, an eleventh-century foundation by Dúnán (Donat), Archbishop of Dublin, which became a parish church in the fifteenth century. As was the case with St. Audoen's Church, whose tower housed the Tanners' Guild, St. Michael's had a guild association with the Corporation of Shoemakers. By the 1790s the church was not thriving, and it had to be rebuilt in the early nineteenth century. However, its proximity to Christ Church meant that it would be taken as the site of its Synod Hall in the 1870s, leaving only the tower standing to this day.

is a basement, and a once-fine stairs leads both down to it and up to the attic.

When built, the hall would have been decorated with paintings of King William III. The tailors would raise a toast to him at dinners that took place not in the hall itself, but in a hostelry named The Phoenix just around the corner in Werburgh Street. At one of these gatherings in 1767, it is recorded that an additional twenty-five toasts were drunk, including one wishing a hot needle and burning thread on all sowers of sedition, and another entreating that 'the needle of distress be ever pointed at the Mock Patriot, whose oratory consists of sophistry … and who would sell his country for interest or discount'.

The Tailors' Hall itself hosted a parliament in 1792, which was known as the 'Back Lane Parliament'. This was a series of meetings organised by Theobald Wolfe Tone, a Protestant patriot who was campaigning for the rights of Catholics to be allowed to vote and have the advantage of trial by jury. He had travelled the country drumming up support, and he succeeded in getting two members from every county to come to the Tailors' Hall and pass a motion recommending such rights. Delegates were sent to London and, to their surprise, were received by King George III. However, it was thirty-seven more years before Daniel O'Connell got his Catholic Emancipation Act through the Westminster Parliament — and what happened to Tone is part of the country's history.

This Back Lane Parliament was the Tailors' Hall's greatest moment of glory, but being the largest public room available in the city, it also served many lesser purposes. The tailors kept the building in repair by letting it out for various functions, which at first included balls and musical events until it was outshone by the Music Hall in nearby Fishamble Street, where Handel's *Messiah* was first performed in 1742. The Tailors' Hall was also let out to other guilds for their own meetings and entertainments, to the Freemasons and, down the years, to various religious organisations who met and prayed there.

The time came for the guilds to disband in the early 1840s. Their assets were sadly sold off, including two tankards from 1680 bought by their present owners, the London Merchant Taylors' Guild. Thereafter, the Back Lane hall was turned into a Protestant boys' school; in turn, it became a whiskey store, a mission hall serving the local community, and, finally, a meeting place for the Legion of Mary. In danger of collapse, it got a reprieve from Dublin Corporation, which agreed to make it safe in 1961, and during the following decade, a number of voluntary societies came together to restore it to something like its original glory. Their action earned the building an Europa Nostra Award for Cultural Heritage in 1981. Finally, three years later, it became very suitably what it fortunately still is: the headquarters of An Taisce, the National Trust for Ireland.

THE ARMS OF
THE TAILORS' GUILD

The Dublin Tailors' Guild possessed its own coat of arms, granted in 1684, most likely by the herald Sir Richard Carney, who had a son and grandson of the same name, also heralds. The father of the first Richard was Edward Carney, a tailor of Dublin.

The shield in the centre features a red pavilion, trimmed in ermine, between two 'maunches' or sleeves (compare the modern French word manchette*). A lamb, possibly indicating patience, is walking on a blue background — representing truth and loyalty — between two bezants (gold coins), representing quality. The two camels as supporters indicate speed and readiness for business, and they also have bezants on their sides. The severed head upon the dish above most likely refers to St. John the Baptist, the patron saint of tailors, who was often depicted semi-naked in the desert. This would fit with the Latin motto,* Nudus et operuistis me *('Naked and you clothed me'), which is based on a line from the Gospel of St. Matthew, 25:36.*

PARLIAMENT HOUSE

arliament as an institution in Ireland goes back to 1264, when the first session was held in Castledermot, County Kildare. Its administrative powers were severely limited by the passing of Poynings' Law in 1494, which dictated that every Act passed in Ireland had first to get the agreement of Royal and Privy Council in London before it could become operative, and had to be agreed in advance. By the seventeenth century, sessions were being held in Dublin Castle, but not on any regular basis. Parliament was abolished under Oliver Cromwell, and there were no sittings held between 1666 and 1685. The passing of the Penal Laws near the end of the seventeenth century meant that political power was now exclusively in the hands of the Protestant aristocracy, particularly those belonging to the Upper House, the House of Lords. From 1692 until the Act of Union in 1800, Catholics could not sit in Parliament, and between 1727 and 1793, they did not even have the right to vote.

Up to the early eighteenth century, the Irish Parliament had no permanent home. It often sat in Dublin Castle, and James II's short-lived Parliament in the late 1680s was held at the King's Inns. And sometimes it sat in Chichester House, a large mansion on College Green (previously Hoggen Green). This had been built at the end of the six-teenth century for Sir George Carew, President of Munster and Lord High Treasurer of Ireland, and was intended as a hospital for disabled soldiers (long before Kilmain-ham Hospital was ever thought of) but, in fact, never used as such. When Chichester House, which accommodated the House of Commons on the ground floor and the House of Lords above, was deemed to be 'very ruinous' and 'not safe inhabiting' by

1700, a committee was set up to look into its demolition and the building of a new, permanent Parliament building on the same site. During the build, the Irish Parliament — which met only every second year — would move to the Blue Coat School on Queen Street.

Thomas Burgh, the Surveyor General, was invited to submit plans for the design of the new structure. He might have thought that his position would have entitled him to be given the job, but it was his more ebullient rival (and successor as Surveyor General) Edward Lovett Pearce who succeeded in getting the contract — to the eternal benefit of the city.

Pearce was of mixed Irish and English stock and had, in fact, worked with Burgh. However, it was his visit to Italy in 1723–1724, and in particular his study of sixteenth-century villas of the Italian architect Andrea Palladio, that prepared him for creating what Dr. Edward McParland describes as 'one of the finest buildings of the time in

KING WILLIAM III AS A ROMAN GENERAL

The equestrian statue of King William III on College Green was a symbol of religious oppression for many Dubliners. It was a substantial work by Grinling Gibbons, a Dutch sculptor commissioned by the city fathers in 1701 to create this monument to the Protestant victor of the Battle of the Boyne. It suffered insults over the years, and you can see here that a guardhouse has been set up next to it for protection. It survived the birth of the Irish Free State by only seven years, and was blown up in 1929. Other statues of royalty were removed from the country in later years and rehomed in England and Australia.

Europe'. It took him just six weeks to work on the general design of this complex structure; further details were doubtless fleshed out later.

His design was innovative, not to say startling: a curved patio giving access to a raised platform on which was built a grand central portico projecting from the flanking Ionic colonnade. Perhaps more surprisingly, the two side walls of the courtyard, partially colonnaded too, opened out onto the street with very tall pedimented arches, as if welcoming the visitors with open arms and neatly enclosing the set-back portico. What is so wonderful about the arrangement of columns in the whole front of the building is the variations of light and shade which they provide, giving constantly new vistas depending on where one stands close to the rusticated granite walls. Everything depends on the

Palladian architecture, that splendid re-use of classical idioms adapted to a modern context, whereas sculptural decoration was confined to the royal coat of arms carved by John Houghton in the portico's pediment.

This magically muscular entrance seems dignified but simple, yet gives little idea of the complexity of the chambers within, which had to house the separate Houses of Commons and Lords, make space for the Speaker (originally William Conolly of Castletown), and allow for the presence of administrative offices. One feature scarcely visible from the street was a central, rather flat, dome above the House of Commons, while the grandiose House of Lords and its appurtenances were slightly off-centre and facing east-west, looking out towards Westmoreland Street. It is this state of development of the Parliament

A LIFT TO THE HOUSE

The tall eastern pedimented arch of Pearce's Parliament House is seen here. A group of sedan-chair men have gathered after conveying members of Parliament and spectators to the opening session of the house – rather like a modern taxi rank. Students from Trinity College were permitted to enter the visitors' gallery, no doubt with the aim of preparing them for a career in politics, but some had to be excluded for bad behaviour: in the bottom right we see carousing undergraduates running back to the refuge of their college nearby.

House around 1760 that is shown in the accompanying drawing.

The English architect James Gandon was employed in 1785–1786, five years after he had started building the Custom House, to provide a new and imposing entrance to rooms close to the House of Lords. Gandon must have been conscious of the magnificence of Pearce's south-facing entrance and, not wanting to distract from it physically, devised a curving wall with niches – but no windows – to wind eastwards along the side of the building before reaching his new portico facing east on to Westmoreland Street. This had a tall Corinthian order, contrasting with Pearce's Ionic, and was decorated with statues of Fortitude,

Justice and Liberty, carved by Gandon's talented sculptor Edward Smyth. To create this new wing, older houses (including Carew's) had to be demolished and land bought to fit in with the enhancing town-planning ideas of the Wide Streets Commission, a body set up in 1757 that was involved in gradually broadening Dame Street downwards from the Castle towards the Parliament building. To provide a certain symmetry to the western side into what is now Foster Place, Gandon was asked to provide an appropriate extension. But interference from others, and the purloining of his plans (which he later found on sale at an auction) meant that the work was carried out by different and lesser designers, this time in Ionic style, in sympathy

THE WIDER CITY

In the distance, the city of Dublin – thanks to Luke Gardiner – has spread north of the river and now includes the tower of the Lying-in Hospital, better known today as the Rotunda. At this time, ships could tie up along the Quays as far as the modern Grattan (then Essex) Bridge. Just a few years later, with the opening of Carlisle (now O'Connell) Bridge and the Custom House, both designed by James Gandon, ships had to stay to the east of the new axis created by Sackville (now O'Connell) and Westmoreland streets. Merchants in the historic core of the city near Dublin Castle were not pleased at this move to the east.

with Pearce's original building.

A fire in 1792 destroyed Pearce's dome and part of his roof, but more extensive changes became necessary after the Parliament voted itself out of existence in the year 1800. The thorny question of what to do with the building after the Union of Great Britain and Ireland was solved three years later when it was decided that the whole complex should become the headquarters of the Bank of Ireland, founded twenty years earlier. (It continued to serve that purpose until the opening of BOI's new headquarters in Baggot Street in the 1970s.) This change of use involved reworking the interior and assimilating the whole House of Commons area into the new banking layout by Francis Johnston. The House of Lords was the only original part of the interior that was left as it was for people to enjoy to this day. In 1809, the Pearce portico was ornamented by further statues of Hibernia, flanked by Fidelity and Commerce, by Edward Smyth.

The amalgam of the work of some of Ireland's greatest architects of the eighteenth and early nineteenth centuries made what is now the Bank of Ireland building into one of the most striking of all the Georgian buildings to decorate the city. Near its entrance once stood Grinling Gibbons's equestrian statue of William III, William of Orange, which, after a number of sporadic disfigurements, finally succumbed to destruction in 1929.

SEDAN CHAIR
ON THE MOVE

This elaborate sedan chair is from the third quarter of the eighteenth century. It is privately owned, rather than available for public hire; the men carrying the young lady may be from the household staff of her father or husband. A simpler sedan chair for public hire is seen in James Malton's 1792 painting of the Tholsel. And in Malton's 1793 view of Charlemont House, we see an example of a shelter built for sedan-chair men.

A tax on sedan chairs granted by an Act of Parliament in 1785 helped to fund the Rotunda Hospital. This included private sedan chairs, which had to be registered. Thirty-one proprietors had addresses in Rutland (now Parnell) Square, and the accounts provide an index of Dublin's wealthiest streets.

The cost of hire related to time and distance, and this was regulated. 'Set-downs', when the passenger halted the chair to talk to someone, would involve extra payment, similar to 'waiting time' with taxis today.

Sedan chairs remained in use until the 1830s and are visible in many paintings depicting Dublin street life in those years.

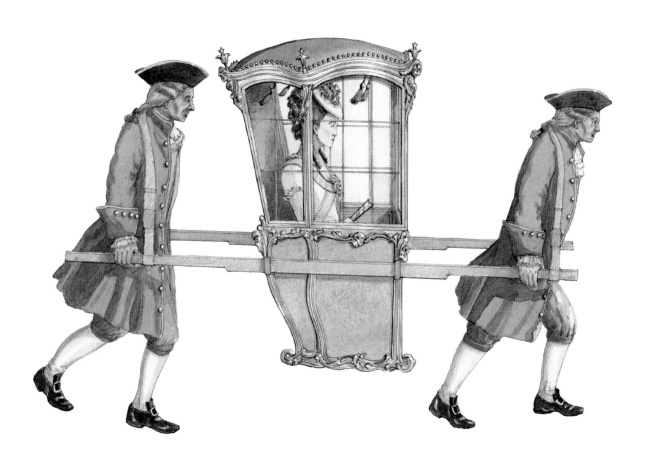

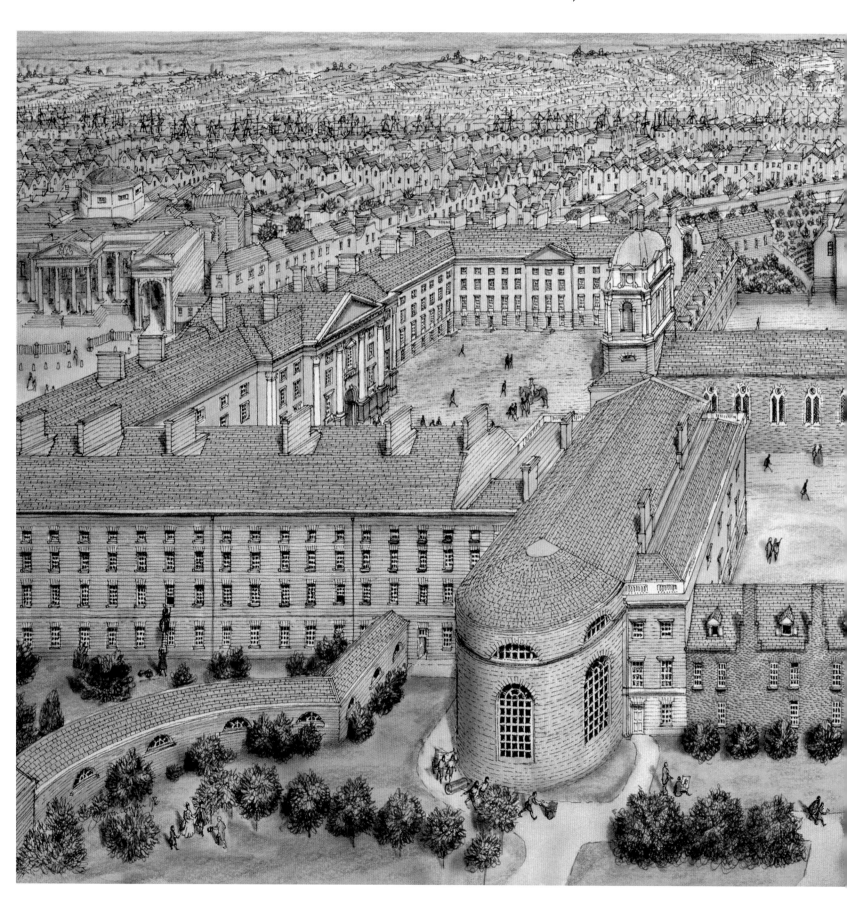

Trinity College is a wonderfully calm oasis at the very centre of the city of Dublin, but the medieval College of All Hallows, which was originally on this spot, was situated quite far east of the capital's heart and hub during the Later Middle Ages, almost lapped by the waters of the River Liffey. Founded in 1592 during the reign of Queen Elizabeth I 'to implant learning, increase civility' and establish the English monarch's new Protestant religion, its buildings were far different from what we see today. In fact, not a single element of the original structures survives, and what we see now — and what the accompanying drawing shows of the college as it was in 1780 — contains virtually nothing that predates the eighteenth century. When it was beginning to evolve into its modern configuration, it was significantly close to Pearce's Parliament building (top left of the main image), a geographical link that helped when it came to getting funds for re-shaping the campus during the eighteenth century.

Probably the most famous, and one of the oldest surviving, of Trinity's buildings is the three-storey library, seen in the bottom right of the main illustration. It was built by Sir Thomas Burgh, a graduate of the college who became Surveyor General in 1700 — succeeding Sir William Robinson, of Royal Hospital, Kilmainham, fame — and began the library twelve years later. It stands proudly as it did three centuries ago, the main exterior difference being that the ground floor arcades, once open, were glazed in the 1890s to provide more space for books. The library's interior is even more famous. Originally it was a long but not very tall hall on the first floor, lined with leather-bound

TRINITY, THEN AND NOW

Those who know Trinity College well will recognise at least two-thirds of the buildings here. On the left is visible part of the single-storey curved way, built around 1760, that leads from Parliament Square to the Provost's House; to the right of it is the rounded end of the Examination Hall, originally designed as a theatre. The red-brick range in the middle of the picture has long since disappeared, the site of the 1937 Reading Room, reserved for postgraduate study. On the right is Sir Thomas Burgh's library, begun in 1712, seen before the nineteenth-century alterations that would encase the building in granite and add a wooden barrel vault to the interior.

books and marble busts. Around 1860, its flat ceiling was removed by the architects Deane & Woodward and replaced with a high barrel vault to create what is now the Long Room, one of the most magnificent interior spaces in the country. In Edward McParland's words, 'What had been superb, the architects made sublime.' The library's greatest treasures, the Books of Armagh, Durrow and, above all, Kells, were formerly displayed here, but these have now been moved down to the ground floor to provide easier access for the thousands of visitors who come to visit every day.

The library formed the southern end of Library Square (more correctly an oblong), the other three sides of which consisted of three-storey ranges with dormer-windowed attics. The only remaining part is the nearer half of the eastern range, seen on the right of the main image,

which may be a decade or so earlier than the library and is the oldest surviving section of the college. Known as the Rubrics, from their red brick, they were curtailed at either end around the mid-nineteenth century, but they still provide rooms for teaching staff and guests. Hidden behind the north-eastern corner of Library Square is the small classical Printing House, built by Richard Castle in 1734.

Roughly where the Campanile of 1852–1855 now stands, the centre of the west side of Library Square was interrupted by the west end of a long chapel, where students had the first of their three compulsory daily prayer visits at six o'clock in the morning. The chapel was accessed under Richard Castle's tall tower opposite the entrance from Dame Street, which was, however, taken down after it was

RICHARD CASTLE'S TOWER, LATER DEMOLISHED FOR REASONS OF SAFETY

THE CHAPEL AT THAT TIME (1780)

THE DINING HALL, BUILT AFTER CASTLE'S FIRST
BUILDING BECAME UNSTABLE

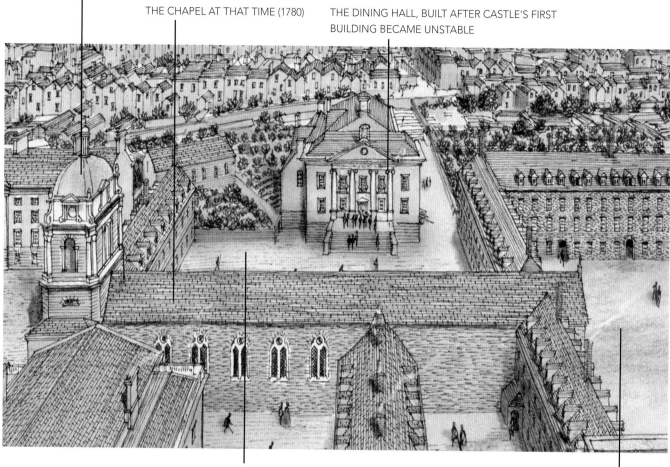

THE SITE OF THE MODERN-DAY CHAPEL, BUILT TO
THE DESIGN OF WILLIAM CHAMBERS IN THE LATE
EIGHTEENTH CENTURY

LIBRARY SQUARE, WHICH HAD RED-BRICK RANGES ON THREE SIDES.
ONLY THE EASTERN RANGE SURVIVES AS THE RUBRICS

found to be too insecure to hold the college's bell. Castle was also responsible for a dining hall that replaced an earlier one but that, in turn, had to be replaced by the present structure after Castle's version fell down in a storm. The subsequent collapse of the dining hall vaults necessitated its total demolition – so that the Printing House remains as Castle's single contribution to the college's architecture. The present dining hall of the 1760s, the pedimented building facing the viewer in the centre of the picture above, was built by the Darley family (quarrymen, later builders and architects) to house the splendid hall where fellows and students dine together on Commons during certain parts of the year.

The removal of the chapel and tower and other adjoining red-brick buildings provided an opportunity to open up the whole front portion of the college grounds and make the old library and Parliament Square into a grandiose open space. This made for the creation of two seemingly twin buildings on either side of Parliament Square, one of which is seen in the main illustration, left of centre in the foreground, as the rounded end of the Examination Hall, which was originally designed as a theatre. It is from the front of this building that the Provost annually announces the names of new Fellows and Scholars amid great pomp and circumstance on Trinity Monday – to loud cheers from the assembled multitude!

After the old hall and the tower standing in front of it had been demolished, the way was open to build a new chapel opposite the Examination Hall. Externally, they were twins based on designs by the famous English architect William Chambers, who was also responsible for the Casino at Marino, arguably the greatest gem of Irish architecture. But Chambers resigned from the job in 1778, and the two buildings were completed before the end of the century by Christopher Myers and his son Graham. Both buildings provide a wonderful classical dignity to the flanks of Parliament Square, leading the eye towards the main college entrance as seen in the detail below. This has a fine four-storey pedimented centre decorated with four tall Corinthian columns rising from

ACCESS TO EDUCATION

The main entrance to Trinity College is seen here in the centre, designed by Theodore Jacobsen, part of the grand architectural scheme that will eventually deliver the very open interior space of the college's historic core that we know today. His two pavilions at either end of the exterior façade are not visible here. In the top left we see Parliament House, where some Trinity students would eventually take their place as members of the House.

the first floor. The same design was repeated on the exterior façade facing onto College Green and opposite the Parliament building. The architect here was the Englishman Theodore Jacobsen, who was already well known for his Foundling Hospital in London. The exterior has a remarkable pavilion at each end, but these are not seen in this interior view of Parliament Square, where Jacobsen's front gate was flanked by the north and south wings (probably the work of Keane and Sanderson, associates of Jacobsen in London).

Leading out from the south-facing side of the south wings in bottom-left of the main picture is a semi-circular way that leads to the Provost's House, built around 1760.

No. 1 Grafton Street is the best address in town and one of the few Georgian houses in the city still used for the purpose for which it was built. The house has its own garden, indicated by the trees on the bottom left, beside which the Fellows had their own garden, since replaced by modern buildings.

The bird's eye view of Trinity College in this picture, which shows us the layout as it was in a map by Byron of around 1780, presents us with a radically different view of the college, then more compartmentalised, but nowadays a wonderful open space framed by the city's finest cluster of classical buildings, assembled in this great centre of learning.

AN EIGHTEENTH-CENTURY STUDENT OF TCD

This young man is clearly from a privileged background and wears a smart green coat and breeches. His under-

graduate academic gown has characteristic square shoulder flaps that hang over at either side. The gown is not

sleeved; he will have to progress through the university to acquire such a distinction. Each stage of the four-year

bachelor's course has a name: Junior Freshman, Senior Freshman, Junior Sophister and Senior Sophister, followed

by graduation. The student holds a mortar board, a square academic cap with a tassel. Depictions of Dublin

students show them wearing their caps up to the mid-nineteenth century, but the tradition nowadays is that men

merely carry their caps while women may actually wear them.

There was some 'town and gown' trouble over the centuries, but Dublin was never dominated by the university in

the way of Oxford, Cambridge or St. Andrews. There were occasional reports of wild young men who enjoyed fights

with the locals, using the heavy keys to their rooms as weapons, but our subject here seems of a milder disposition. He

may one day sit in the Irish Parliament of Grattan, though he may also see the House dissolved by the Act of Union

in 1800.

We can all too easily get carried away by the architectural beauty of Georgian Dublin, looking with envy at the beautiful clothes that not only the women but also the men wore, and the upper-class lifestyle of parties in fabulously furnished houses. But have a thought for the poorer city denizens, who would, of course, have made up the majority of the population. Nowhere was this contrast between rich and poor more evident than in the medical treatment meted out to the various categories of patients. Perhaps worst hit were the women, who had to experience the death of so many of their offspring during childbirth.

One of those whose social conscience was pricked by this disastrous state of affairs was Dr. Bartholomew Mosse, son of a Protestant clergyman from Maryborough, now Portlaoise. His parents sent him to Dublin to become an apprentice to a surgeon and, like many who were to follow him in centuries to come, he went abroad for further medical experience, serving as a doctor to the British troops stationed on the Balearic island of Menorca. He later visited hospitals in England and France — most notably the Hôtel-Dieu de Paris, perhaps the most active of Europe's maternity hospitals at the time — where he quickly realised the pitfalls that lay in wait for pregnant women in large wards. On his return to Dublin, Mosse determined that his fellow countrywomen would not be exposed to similar danger, and to puerperal fever in particular. With his newly won obstetrical expertise, he decided in 1745 to convert a virtually abandoned theatre in what is now South Great George's Street into

PLEASURE GARDENS

The carriage seen in the bottom right of this detail belongs to one of the titled patrons of the Lying-in Hospital, who has brought his family to view the chapel – where patrons' coats of arms were painted on the walls – and to enjoy the gardens. The general public enter the pleasure gardens on foot by way of a walled entry, seen here leading diagonally from the left. To the left we see the private garden of a house that stood alone for several decades before disappearing by 1800, leaving the Rotunda in sole possession of the southern side of the square. The gray roof in the upper right of the image belongs to the Long Room, where refreshments could be taken.

a small-scale maternity hospital. There, within the next twelve years, he helped to deliver more than four thousand babies. But his experience made him realise that the care offered in a comparatively simple three-storey house needed to be vastly improved, and so the idea gathered in his mind to build a much grander hospital that would serve rich and poor in equal measure and bring more children safely into the world.

To augment the profits from his own private midwifery practice, Mosse had to become a businessman in order to make this dream come true. With the aid of his numerous friends (some of whose wives he had probably treated), he bought a four-acre site on what is now Parnell Square. He first busied himself with preparing and extensively planting a garden which rivalled (and was probably modelled on) Vauxhall Gardens in London. By charging entry fees

for those who could afford it, it became a popular place of pastime; it also helped to pay for his new hospital.

Mosse sought the assistance of one of the most famous architects of the time in Ireland: Richard Castle or Cassells, a German of Jewish origin whose other triumphs included the mansions of Russborough and Carton, as well as Leinster House on the south side of the Liffey. Over several tavern meetings, the pair drew up the plans for the new hospital, which was to be homelier than the two existing hospitals (other than his own) in the city: the Royal Hospital, Kilmainham, and Dr. Steevens' Hospital.

A PLACE OF POLITE RESORT

In the foreground is the tall, copper-domed tower of the hospital, said to have been planned as an observatory. It is surmounted with a gilded cradle, crown and ball that cost the huge sum of £137. On the green beyond, bowling matches are in progress, and in the centre on the terrace above is the 'orchestra', an eight-columned circular temple where musicians would play. Behind the thickly planted area, today the site of the Garden of Remembrance, is one of the grandest ranges of domestic buildings in Dublin. At its centre is the stone-fronted Charlemont House, designed by William Chambers and built in 1765. Two houses to the left, number 24 was owned by Frederick Trench MP, who developed the idea of the assembly rooms that were later added to the Rotunda. The five-bay house at the far right end of the terrace was demolished to make way for a neo-Gothic Presbyterian church in the 1860s. The house next to it, number 18, is now the Dublin Writers' Museum.

Both of these were organised around a central courtyard; the new hospital was designed to be square but without the courtyard in the centre. Castle was a devotee of the sixteenth-century Italian architect Andrea Palladio, and he based his designs on Palladio's clever adaptation of the old Roman style to Renaissance taste.

The main front of the hospital, facing onto Parnell Street, is a three-storey, eleven-bay building, with a Doric portico projecting out in the two upper floors. As if pro-

tecting it, a Doric colonnade curves outwards on either side towards the street, providing an area in front of the hospital where, in the eighteenth century, the carriages of the gentlemen and their ladies could come and go without causing a traffic jam. The north side of the building, facing the garden and not normally on view today, was more restrained but equally supplied with projecting colonnaded quadrants. Dominating the view of both the front and back of the building was an unexpectedly tall tower, said to have been originally planned by Mosse for use as an observatory.

In addition to raising money through a lottery, Mosse wanted to extract cash from the rich citizens of the capital by dazzling them with a chapel, which now looks out through nineteenth-century stained glass onto Parnell Street. This took up the height of two floors, led up to by a grand staircase with a beautiful stucco ceiling in order to make the maximum impression – as it still does. The chapel is probably the finest eighteenth-century church interior in the country and an absolute joy to visit. (Access is currently by appointment only on Wednesday mornings.) Contrasting with the restrained ornament of the old entrance hall beneath it (with its bust of Mosse by Van Nost), the chapel is a riot of rococo stuccowork, among the earliest in the city, executed by the masterly Belgian

stuccodore Bartholomew Cramillion. The chapel is two storeys high, with a gallery supported by pillars running around three of the walls. Above are lunettes bearing figures of Faith, Hope and Charity, flanked by terms, the busts of playful putti (so suitable for a maternity hospital), who also guard the tablets of the Ten Commandments above the organ. The surrounds of the east window support the Adoration of the Paschal Lamb, adorned by flanking angels with the backing of a curtain.

The chapel must have wowed visitors when it first opened to the public in 1762, and its decorative delights must have had the desired effect of extracting money from those who came along to hear the charity sermons in such exuberant surroundings. Castle died before the building was completed in 1757, and it was John Ensor who put the finishing touches to it. It was he who created the adjoining

A ROUNDED EXPERIENCE

The Rotunda that eventually gave its name to the Lying-in Hospital was built of brick. It is shown here rendered to give the impression of stone, but it would later have a more durable and convincing cladding, including Coade stone panels possibly by Edward Smyth. His excellent sculptural work adorned several major public buildings in the city, most notably the Custom House. To the right are single-storey refreshment rooms that also opened onto the eastern side of Rutland (now Parnell) Square. This corner of the square is well documented by artists of the Georgian period.

round building – the Rotunda – which gave its name to the whole hospital when completed in 1767. This was another remarkable building within the complex. Originally built in red brick, it had a low, domed ceiling spanning almost twenty-five metres of the interior without any internal support. It was entered from the street by a low building (some think designed by James Gandon) and provided a splendid venue for concerts organised to support the hospital financially, adding immeasurably to the musical life of Dublin. What we see of the Rotunda today – it is now The Ambassador Event Centre – got a cladding of Coade stone bucrania, or bull's skulls, thought to have been the work of the famous sculptor Edward Smyth, who embellished so many other Georgian buildings in Dublin with his statuary. The entertainment element of this group of buildings is maintained today by the Gate Theatre, which opened in 1930 on the upper floor of what was originally the supper room.

It is a remarkable tribute to Bartholomew Mosse that his tireless work as an obstetrician, entrepreneur and concert impresario, which led to his death in 1759 at the age of only forty-seven, has continued to the present day, when the head gynaecologist is still called the Master, as was the case in Mosse's time. This was the very first purpose-built maternity hospital in these islands, and, even if a little outdated for modern medicine, the Rotunda is still looked upon with great affection, not only by those who have had their babies there but also by the thousands of gynaecology students who have thronged to the hospital down the years from many parts of the globe.

One of Mosse's methods of fundraising was to hold lotteries and, at one stage, he was even imprisoned because he was accused of embezzling some of the profits. He had to hide for a time in the Welsh mountains, to escape those who were trying to make life difficult for this philanthropic man. But he also became a property speculator and built a number of the first houses in Cavendish Row and Parnell (formerly Rutland) Square; number 9 was built for Mosse himself in the year before the hospital opened. While some of the houses in Parnell Square have been rebuilt or replaced, most of the surviving examples date from the 1760s. The finest building of them all – and the only one of stone – was that built in 1765 for the Earl of Charlemont by William Chambers (who also designed the Casino at Marino for him). It was at the very centre of the north side of the square and looked directly across the gardens to Mosse's hospital on the other side. It was commented upon very handsomely by the Rev. Thomas Campbell, who said of it in 1778 that 'Lord Charlemont's cannot be called a great house, but nothing could be more elegant'. It is now Dublin City Gallery The Hugh Lane.

THE CEILING OF THE ROTUNDA CHAPEL

The plasterwork of the Rotunda chapel was originally intended to be accompanied by paintings in the four corner panels. Cramillion's work was subsequently part-painted with semi-naturalistic colours. While inanimate subjects such as fruit and foliage were coloured, human forms were left white. In this drawing a small part of the work has been rendered back to how the plasterwork would have appeared without the colouring.

THE ROYAL COLLEGE
OF SURGEONS

1750–2010

At around the same time that the Duke of Ormonde was donating the Phoenix Park to the north-side citizens of Dublin, the city's Corporation was making the first moves in 1663/1664 to have houses built on St. Stephen's Green on the south side. It comprised about sixty acres of grazing land, and the city fathers decided to lease out ninety-six plots around a central green. These were of various sizes, but unexpectedly large for a local authority, which, however, gave Dubliners a taste for bigger houses that was to continue for more than a century. Unlike many of the Green's later inhabitants, who often bore titles, those who initially took the plots were common folk – a butcher, a mason and a surveyor among others – and they accepted the strictures laid down that they should make their houses two storeys high and roof them with slates. Some of these were later called 'Dutch Billys' (named after King William III, victor at the Battle of the Boyne), and can be seen here in the opposite picture with undulating, rather barock, skyline profiles topping their gables end-on to the street.

In less than a century, the Green became one of Dublin's most fashionable addresses for aristocrats and church dignitaries, and the houses – particularly on three sides – provide fine examples of stucco work, from the rare and beautiful rococo style to the more neo-classical Adamesque patterns. All four sides of the Green now have gaps in their original teeth, as it were, with demolitions followed by modern refills right up to the present day. Yet the original charm of the central Green is still preserved

for us, the gardens well flowered and looked after by the Office of Public Works. Eighteenth-century engravings show it to have been a place for fireworks and in which the gentry would go walking to show off their latest finery. One of them, the famous and outspoken Mrs. Delany, a niece of Lord Lansdowne's, claimed proudly that the Green 'may be preferred justly to any square in London'.

It is the west side of the Green that has changed most down the years, with only two houses left of its eighteenth-century splendour – but what comes nearest to it is the early nineteenth-century centrepiece, the Royal College of Surgeons in Ireland. Its location is perhaps appropriate as the Green gets its name from a medieval church and hospital for lepers dedicated to the first Christian martyr,

St. Stephen. The surgeons were once allied with the barbers (which is why they are called 'Mr.' rather than 'Dr.'), but that came to an end when the surgeons got their own charter in 1784. They lacked a premises that they could call their own – or funds to go and build one – yet they slowly got over their problems by acquiring a disused hall. The value of having surgeons to tend the wounded during the Napoleonic wars convinced the government of the day to give the nascent college a large grant with which to build a new house of its own. The land acquired to do so was, curiously, part of an old Quaker graveyard, which was given to the college only on the understanding that it would not build on a particular part of it. So, at the corner of York Street, a new building was erected. It was designed

1810

Edward Parke's Surgeons' Hall now stands on the site of the Quaker burial ground, while the two houses on the adjoining plots, which we saw in 1750, have been demolished. The Irish nationalist and republican Robert Emmet was born in 1778 into an Anglo-Irish Protestant family in the house to the right of Glover's Alley. His father was a court physician. The horse and dray could have belonged to one of the three major breweries of the time: Thwaites, Andrews or Guinness, this last being more than fifty years in business by this time.

by Edward Parke, a competent if not brilliant architect who owed a number of his commissions to his friendship with John Foster, Chancellor of the Irish Exchequer in Westminster at the time. The son of an architect, Parke's only other well-known building in Dublin was the Commercial Building in Dame Street (now demolished and replaced by a copy – but at right angles!). What Parke produced, at a time when the wealthy were gradually moving their base to London, was an attractive if not very large three-bay pedimented building giving on to Stephen's Green. It was longer on the side adjoining York Street, respecting the promise given to the Quakers.

Decorative and compact as Parke's building was, it was just not big enough for the rising number of students,

and, only fifteen years after its completion, the college realised that it needed a larger building. For whatever reason, Parke was not given the job; it fell, instead, to William Murray, who had been employed earlier by the better-known architect Francis Johnston. The demolition of the neighbouring 'Dutch Billys' gave Murray space to erect an equally two-storeyed pedimented building with large, deep windows on the first floor and a doorway in the centre that is used nowadays only for special occasions, as the main entrance to the college is around the corner in York Street. Like Parke's façade, it had granite blocks on the ground floor and columns between the windows above, but Murray's frontage now had seven bays. The pediment of the enlarged structure was adorned with statues by John Smyth, the son of Gandon's favourite sculptor Edward Smyth, who had created the statues for the Custom House and the eastern portico of the Parliament Building on College Green. The royal arms are the central feature of the pediment, which is flanked above by the figures of Athena, the Hellenes' goddess of wisdom, and Hygeia, the Greek goddess of health, while above the point of the pediment stands Asclepius, the god of healing, who gets further exposure in the form of the head above the entrance doorway on Stephen's Green.

From its poor financial resources more than two hundred years ago, the college came on in leaps and bounds in the twentieth century, when major fundraising efforts allowed the addition of a new School of Medicine along York Street, and more building is currently underway on the opposite side of the same street, all with the intention of allowing student numbers to increase and their facilities to improve. By 1978, there were nearly seven hundred students, three-quarters of whom came from outside Ireland — from more than sixty different countries — bringing in much-appreciated development capital. In 2010, the two-hundredth anniversary of its home on St. Stephen's Green, the college was given the honour of being able to award its own degrees, as universities do. It was perhaps no surprise that, at around the same time, it began to expand even beyond the bounds of Europe with the setting up of schools in Asia and the Middle East.

1827

The Surgeons' Hall has been extended and is now called the Royal College of Surgeons. It occupies the whole space between York Street and Glover's Alley. This was the scene of a gun battle during the Easter Rising of 1916 between British troops and Irish insurgents under Michael Mallin and Countess Markievicz. She was born Constance Georgine Gore-Booth at Buckingham Gate in London, the elder daughter of the Arctic explorer and adventurer Sir Henry Gore-Booth, 5th Baronet.

2010

The flag of the Royal College of Surgeons in Ireland is seen atop the building. It consists of a red saltire with a severed hand in its centre. Above is a ground of ermine with a harp and crown upon it, placed between two fleams (devices for bloodletting). The flag draws on the arms granted in 1645 to the Dublin Guild of Barber-Surgeons. The building on the right is 124 St. Stephen's Green, which has held offices since 2005. It stretches a considerable distance along Glover's Alley and adjoins the luxurious Fitzwilliam Hotel. These buildings symbolise the economic boom of the early 2000s. Construction began on the Luas tram system in 2000, and the first working trams returned to the streets of Dublin on June 30th, 2004, with a second line in operation from September of the same year.

A NAVAL SURGEON OF THE POST-NAPOLEONIC ERA

This experienced surgeon is contemplating his next patient. Such men had to act very quickly when perform-

ing amputations. They might have had the assistance of two strong men to hold the patient, but the key

was the ability to circle round the limb with the saw and cauterise the wound, all in a matter of seconds.

Rum was the nearest thing to an anaesthetic for the amputee. The surgeon is shown here with a set of

eighteenth-century surgical instruments from the collection of Trinity College, Dublin.

TRA
COMM

THE CUSTOM HOUSE

The centre of social, commercial, ecclesiastical and legal life in Dublin during the first half of the eighteenth century lay largely in the area around Dublin Castle and Christ Church Cathedral, the core of the old Viking town. That was reinforced in the 1770s with the building of the superbly detailed Royal Exchange, now the City Hall, at the gates of Dublin Castle and the top of Parliament Street. It was reached from north of the Liffey over Essex (now Grattan) Bridge, built in the 1750s as the lowest bridge before the river flowed into the Irish Sea. Close by, roughly where the Clarence Hotel now stands, was the Old Custom House, built by Thomas Burgh early in the century. Its location was fine for local businessmen but inconvenient for boatmen; the waters were shallow, forcing them to moor their boats parallel to one another out towards the centre of the river.

Ideas were, however, floating around to move commercial activity further downstream to the east. After all, there was the new College Green axis of the Parliament Building of around 1730 and the façade of Trinity College, completed around 1760. In addition, there were the interests of landowning developers such as Luke Gardiner. He wanted to build houses on his plots in Sackville (now O'Connell) Street, even though there was at the time no bridge to connect it to the south side, where the Duke of Leinster built his mansion (now the Dáil and Seanad) between Kildare Street and Merrion Square in 1745, taunting others to follow his lead.

Worth bearing in mind, too, is an organisation named the Wide Streets Commission, set up in 1757 to achieve what its name implied. To it we owe the breadth of

PEOPLE AND BUSINESS ON THE MOVE

This area to the east of the Custom House has changed completely since 1840. Just four years later, the railway terminus now called Connolly Station was opened in the upper right-hand corner, bringing the rail line to Drogheda and later connecting with the north-east of the country. The Loopline Bridge was added in 1891 to connect this terminus with Westland Row and beyond to the south. Dublin's Dart trains use the Loopline's engineering, and now trams have returned to the area in the form of the Luas system, which passes by the Custom House on its east-west city-centre route. The Old Dock to the right of the Custom House in this image has since been filled in. It has become Dublin's financial centre, reflecting the future of many older buildings to the east of this area.

O'Connell Street, Dame Street and the triangle formed by D'Olier and Westmoreland streets, and the present College Green. Among the Commissioners in 1780 was not only Luke Gardiner (who stood to gain financially by the new broader thoroughfares) but influential people such as Lord Carlow (later Earl of Portarlington) and Gardiner's brother-in-law John Beresford, an important revenue commissioner. This latter pair were visitors to the London salon of the painter Paul Sandby, who introduced them to the architect James Gandon, first pupil of the great William Chambers. Beresford, who became Chairman of the Revenue Commissioners in 1780, decided that Gandon was just the right man to build a new Custom House farther downstream on the other bank of the Liffey, which he felt would give a helpful fillip to maritime trade in providing easier and speedier

customs clearance to incoming mariners. Knowing that there would be considerable opposition from the merchants trading farther upstream around the Old Custom House, he clandestinely introduced Gandon to Ireland and to Dublin, a city which he was to ornament so brilliantly over the following quarter century.

When Gandon arrived in 1781, he quickly realised that he had a gargantuan task ahead of him; the site he was to build upon could be covered by the sea at the time of the spring tides. He resolutely set about the task of making foundations with the aid of stout piles of Baltic timber rammed into the ground and reinforced with bricks and mortar, creating a platform which removed any danger of flooding. The foundation stone was secretly laid in August 1781. When the furious merchants upstream discovered that Beresford was now definitely going to go ahead with his plans, they gave the populace whiskey and gingerbread in the hope that they would riot. Instead, they drank and ate their fill, swam in Gandon's trenches – and went home happy.

What arose above the foundations over the next decade became one of Dublin's most iconic and admired buildings. Beresford may have been out of step with Henry Grattan, whose Parliament (1782–1800) coincided with Dublin's most glittering period of independence, but his building added to its sparkle. The building is 115 metres long and almost 64 metres wide, the main emphasis being on the two long sides – one facing northwards towards Gardiner Street, with a semi-circular garden in front, and providing the main entrance; the other facing the river, with only a token entrance that is now no longer used. Both long sides were dominated by a portico joined to corner pavilions by arcades on the ground floor and windows on the floor above. Though the dome over the centre of the building was originally fairly flat, Gandon later made it very much taller, suitably topping it off with a statue of Commerce.

One of the most striking features of the building is the richness of its sculptural decoration. Anyone passing nearby on the railway bridge can see the remarkable coat of arms – consisting of a lion and a unicorn on either side, a crown on top, and, in the centre, not the royal arms one might expect but the harp of Ireland – on the east end of the front of the building. They proudly show off the independence the country had recently achieved in Grattan's Parliament. This work was carried out by Gandon's favourite sculptor, Edward Smyth, born perhaps in County Meath. His statues are carefully worked out to be seen correctly from below, and they can look rather strange when viewed at eye level (see p. 121). Smyth's quality of work, but also his sense of humour, comes out in the keystones of the building, which show human faces flanked by fish and other marine creatures, representing the major rivers of Ireland. A number of these were used on banknotes in the early years of the

GEORGIAN LANDMARKS

Gardiner Street Lower, one of the original approaches to the Custom House's 'business entrance', is seen receding up the slope into the distance here. Farther away, we can make out some of the landmarks of Georgian Dublin: on the left is the tower of the Rotunda Hospital, and in the middle is the striking tower of St. George's Church, Hardwicke Place, by the architect Francis Johnston. In fifty years' time, the Loopline Bridge will cut across this image.

State; it is said that the higher the value of the legal tender note, the greater the smile on the river chosen. Added to the faces we find the figure of the Atlantic Ocean, perhaps indicating Ireland's claim to be allowed to service Britain's colonies on the other side of the ocean, after free-trade restrictions had earlier been lifted.

The drawing here shows the building as it was half a century after its construction, but the Custom House has not, alas, survived exactly as Gandon left it. In May 1921, Michael Collins and the Dublin Brigade of the IRA set fire to the building, which burned for five days, leaving part of the structure a mass of rubble. It was eight years before reconstruction began, and not without alterations affecting the central part of the building – most noticeably in replacing the original imported Portland stone with native Ardbraccan limestone in the masonry supporting the dome. Another change was the replacement by windows of the niches on the first floor of the south face overlooking the river.

Despite the necessary changes to reconstruct the building internally for use as modern offices, it still remains the most admired of Dublin's buildings. Along with Gandon's Four Courts and the Bank of Ireland to which he also contributed, it revitalised the centre of Dublin in neo-classical style, more so than London itself, to which city so many Irish peers and landowners had removed themselves after the Act of Union came into force in 1801. Later that century, of course, the vista of the Custom House from upstream was interrupted by the creation of the Loopline Bridge necessary to connect railway stations north and south of the Liffey. In the 1960s, it was to be dwarfed by the construction of the seventeen-floor Liberty Hall. The best view to be got nowadays is from east of the railway bridge on the opposite bank of the Liffey, from where the majesty of this wonderful building can be most easily appreciated.

KEYSTONE
PORTRAYING
THE RIVER LIFFEY

The excellent sculptures by Edward Smyth on the Custom House show how care-fully he thought about where on the building his work would appear, and how it would be viewed. On the left, the carving is seen face-on, as if one is viewing it while standing at the top of a ladder; on the right is the same work, but seen from below. A face that is too long is altered to fit the norms of beauty. As with the other keystones representing the rivers of Ireland, the fruits, flowers and crops produced along the course of the River Liffey are shown.

TARY
TERS

THE ROYAL HOSPITAL,
KILMAINHAM

The seventeenth century was one of the most turbulent in this country's history. It opened with the Battle of Kinsale in 1601, followed by the Flight of the Earls in 1607, which saw the departure of the flower of Gaelic society from an Ireland being taken over by an English administration that thereafter began settling the confiscated lands of Ulster — the reverberations of which are still with us. The mid-century years saw the arrival of Cromwell and his Parliamentarians, who wreaked havoc outside the capital in Drogheda and elsewhere. Dublin was spared the mayhem because James Butler, later to become the first Duke of Ormonde, relinquished the city in 1647, tried unsuccessfully to re-take it two years later, then left it to Cromwell's men, who caused no bloodshed in the capital. Instead, the city suffered from three separate waves of bubonic plague in the 1650s, when many of its half-timbered houses were demolished, leaving the way open to start the great Dublin tradition of building in stone and brick from the mid-1660s onwards.

A new era dawned for Dublin with the re-emergence of the Duke of Ormonde after the restoration of the English monarchy in 1660 under Charles II. Ormonde would have been a loyal supporter of the Stuart kings, and he was duly rewarded in 1662 by being made the king's viceroy in Ireland. He re-entered the city amongst great jubilation, bringing with him a new confidence that he passed on to the citizens — or at least to the Protestant citizens, as religious toleration for the Catholics was denied. A man of culture, Ormonde was responsible for a great resurgence in Dublin's drama scene

The influence of Paris's Hôtel des Invalides is particularly felt in the courtyard of Royal Hospital, Kilmainham. The tower and spire were finished by 1701, some seventeen years after the hospital opened.

in setting up the Smock Alley Theatre in 1661 and, later in the decade, giving the city one of the largest public spaces in Europe – the Phoenix Park – where a seven-mile-long wall enclosed a large herd of deer, some of whose probable descendants still roam its pastures today. It was particularly during Ormonde's third term as Viceroy (1677 to 1685) that Dublin saw an increase in population to an estimated 50,000, including doubtless some recent arrivals from the countryside and from abroad, which seems to have gone hand-in-hand with an increase in trade.

The city became more upper-class in its lifestyle. Orders were being placed for furniture, glass and silver, and there was a remarkable rise in the printing trade, par-

tially inspired no doubt by the prestige which Ormonde was bestowing on the city. One of his important, if not very long-lasting, achievements was the building of the Tholsel, a two-storey structure near the corner of Nicholas Street and Skinner's Row (now Christchurch Place). Like the present City Hall, when first built its purpose was to act as a meeting place for merchants and others, where business could be transacted and where the city assembly and its officers could meet on the upper floor. Its façade was decorated with statues of England's two Charles kings, I and II, which were removed to the crypt of Christ Church Cathedral after the Tholsel was demolished in 1809. Its disappearance left only one major public building of the seventeenth century to survive in the city – the remarkable Royal Hospital in Kilmainham, which also owes its very existence to Ormonde, whose last great achievement as Viceroy it was.

The idea of a hospital for army veterans had already emerged in 1677 during the vice-regal term of the Earl of Essex, who had sent Lord Granard to London to seek funds for the project, but it was the Duke of Ormonde who really pushed the idea forward. The site chosen was part of the extended Phoenix Park, which the Duke had already donated to the State, so its acquisition presented no problems. It was on a slight rise less than two miles west of the city centre, which could be seen from it. The name Kilmainham comes from a church or monastery associated with an early Irish saint named Maighneann, dating back to the seventh century. Perhaps associated with it is an unusual stone cross-shaft of early medieval date, traditionally associated with a son of Brian Boru's, which can be seen in the adjoining Bully's Acre Cemetery. The Knights Hospitallers had a foundation to the west of the present Royal Hospital which once acted as an almshouse and a hospital there, so it was appropriate that Ormonde's site should continue the tradition of caring for the sick.

It was certainly Ormonde who was able to get King Charles II's agreement for the building and who laid the foundation stone in 1680. It was planned to serve three hundred war veterans – at the time the army is reported to have had four hundred 'old and unserviceable men' – and the veterans were to be offered accommodation, recreational facilities and food (bread, three pints of beer, one

THE CHAPEL AND GOVERNOR'S LODGINGS

The exterior of the chapel is seen on the left, with its curved and lead-lined roof for the east window. In the centre is the four-columned, pedimented main entrance, leading to the great hall and vestibule, which look northwards over the sloping ground towards the River Liffey. To the right are the governor's lodgings, and we can see a separate entrance, one bay in from the right, for the governor's family. This entrance has since been removed.

MATURING GARDENS

James Malton's view, with the title 'Old Soldiers
Hospital, Kilmainham', is dated February, 1794, and
dedicated to General Cunninghame, Commander-
in-Chief of the Army and Governor of the Hospital.
Malton's view shows the building over a hundred years
after it opened, and it is clear from both his image and
ours – set just a few years before, in 1780 – that the
trees in the gardens have not kept their seventeenth-
century formality. In fact, it will take until the 1980s for
the original appearance of the terraces and the large
parterre below them to be restored.

pound of beef or mutton, and half a pound of cheese; the officers being better fed). An infirmary was added in 1684.

The man chosen to design the building was William Robinson, then Surveyor General in Ireland. His only precedent was Les Invalides in Paris, begun in 1670, and Kilmainham could claim to have been ahead of the game in these islands in being earlier than the similar Pensioners' Foundation in Chelsea, London. What Robinson achieved in his design was the greatest secular gem of pre-Georgian Dublin. Forming a square, it is three storeys both inside and out, with ground-floor rooms for the veteran soldiers not too good on their legs, first-floor rooms for former officers, while the top floor, with dormer windows in the roof, was reserved for the more agile veterans able to climb the stairs. The tall chimney stacks indicate the former presence of fireplaces to keep the inmates warm.

At the centre of each side was an entrance doorway, three of them beautifully decorated in high relief with floral swags, a portrait-like head and an array of contemporary (and even ancient) arms and armour, all probably carved by a French Huguenot sculptor named Jacques Tabary. The north doorway, facing down towards the Liffey, was the primary entrance. It was chosen because it gave access to the main room of the building, the great hall with vestibule, above which a tower with steeple were later added. On entering the central courtyard today, one is struck by the pedimented decorated gable that stresses the importance of the centre of the north wing. The north doorway is decorated not with the arms of the king, but of the Duke of Ormonde; King Charles II does, however, get his place of prominence by having the intertwined Cs of his name decorating the doorway of the south side of the courtyard.

KILMAINHAM CHAPEL *CIRCA* 1849

This is the only true baroque church remaining in Ireland, and, in the words of Dr. Edward McParland, 'the decorative luxuriance of the chapel is startling'. The great east window, seen in the drawing here, is partially filled with stained glass presented by Queen Victoria after her visit in 1849. But the chapel's greatest joy is the exquisite woodwork decoration, also carved by Tabary. The ceiling was full of decoration that was so heavy it had to be taken down and replaced by a *papier mâché* reproduction. The chapel was not completed until 1687, whereas the main building was ready to receive the veterans three years earlier.

Entering the courtyard is a wonderful experience, with an open arcade or loggia on three sides (originally part of the fourth as well). It gave the veterans the opportunity to walk around and get a breath of fresh air even if it was raining. But most of their time would probably have been spent indoors, sitting on benches around the walls of the great hall where, in later times, mementoes and trophies of past battles and arms were put on permanent display. The great hall was flanked on its western side by the lodgings of the hospital's governor, and on its eastern side by the finest room in the whole complex — the Baroque Chapel, which, even before it was built, raised hopes that it would be 'one of the finest chapels consecrated the King has in his dominions'. (See p. 129.)

The total cost of building the Royal Hospital, Kilmainham, was £25,000; not surprisingly, double the original estimate. Ormonde did not skimp, and he ensured that his family would be represented on the board of governors. William Robinson was duly made auditor and registrar of the hospital. Though later accused of fraud in other dealings, he will, however, be otherwise remembered for having created Charles Fort in Kinsale and Marsh's Library in Dublin. He returned to the hospital as governor from 1697 to 1707; by then the hospital had had its greatest intake of pensioners after the Battle of Aughrim in 1691 — more than four times the number originally planned for.

The hospital continued to serve its purpose until 1927, when it was closed down. The remaining pensioners were sent to its counterpart in Chelsea, where the royal arms that once decorated the Kilmainham hospital are now displayed. Thereafter, it became a repository for items from the National Museum, including a voluminous statue of Queen Victoria now in Sydney. But the building was already beginning to decay for lack of proper maintenance. At one stage it was suggested that it would be a suitable place for a university, while others thought that it would be a wonderful place to house the Dáil and Seanad, but these plans never came to fruition. Restoration work began in earnest in the 1970s, and by 1985, it became the National Centre for Culture and the Arts. In 1986, the Office of Public Works received a Europa Nostra award for its conservation work. In 1991, while Dublin was celebrating its year as European City of Culture, the hospital was finally given its present designation, as a new Museum of Modern Art for Ireland.

A KILMAINHAM
VETERAN

For veterans of the many wars in the eighteenth and nineteenth centuries, to have ended their days in the Royal

Hospital, Kilmainham, must have been something of a dream. Daily life would have been a gentle reminder

of army routine. There were only two such institutions in these islands, the counterpart to Kilmainham being

the Royal Hospital Chelsea in London, opened in 1692. These two hospitals catered for 'in-pensioners',

but the majority of soldiers pensioned out of the army were 'out-pensioners', living at their own addresses

and receiving a pension. This Kilmainham pensioner is from the later nineteenth century, and his uniform

is identical to that at Chelsea.

W & DER

HENRIETTA STREET AND THE KING'S INNS

circa 1830

Henrietta Street, off Bolton Street, was named after the wife of Charles Paulet, second Duke of Bolton, who was King George I's Lord Lieutenant in Ireland from 1717 to 1720. This gives us an inkling of when building might have started in what were then virtually green fields on the north side of the Liffey. Whatever buildings may have stood there at the time do not appear to have had a long life, as three are known to have been demolished a decade later to make room for a single large house for Hugh Boulter, Archbishop of Armagh. These were later, in turn, replaced by the present King's Inns Library in 1825–1828 (seen bottom left in the accompanying picture).

But the person responsible for laying out the street we see today was Luke Gardiner, a man of apparently humble beginnings who, through hard work, banking and an advantageous marriage – and doubtless not a little graft as well – amassed a considerable fortune. This allowed him to become one of the first major Dublin speculators of the eighteenth century. His name is still preserved in Gardiner Street, but his most notable achievement was the creation of the Mall that would later become O'Connell Street.

To make his mark on Henrietta Street in the late 1720s, Gardiner built a large house for himself which currently bears the number 10 (seen here at the top of the street, on the right). Curiously, none of the houses had numbers until 1775, and these were changed to provide the present set in 1845. Needless to say, Gardiner's mansion had one of the largest frontages on to the street, the appearance of which, however, has changed considerably over time. Gardiner added an adjoining house for his son

ALL CHANGE FOR THE ROYAL CANAL

On the left, beyond the red-brick houses, we see the Royal Canal harbour; it was linked by a spur that joined the main canal to the north. It opened in the first years of the nineteenth century. A substantial aqueduct was needed to bring the canal over the road at Constitution Hill: this can be seen on the right, the Foster Aqueduct. In 1845, the new Midland and Great Western Railway Company bought the entire Royal Canal and its harbours, and by 1848, a rail service was running from this site to Mullingar; the Broadstone Station was built in 1850. In 1878, part of the canal spur was filled in to provide a forecourt for the station, and the rest of the spur was filled in by the end of the 1930s. Broadstone itself closed in 1937 and survives as a bus depot. The Foster Aqueduct was removed in 1951 to allow road-widening.

in 1755, which had its front door beneath the Venetian window on the first floor.

But architecturally of greater importance is its neighbour, number 9 (seen here in part on the bottom right), with its red-brick upper storeys surmounting the rusticated ground floor. There are good reasons for thinking that Edward Lovett Pearce, Ireland's greatest Palladian architect of the eighteenth century, was heavily involved in the design of most, if not all, of this house. It was closely modelled on the London home of Richard Boyle, Lord Burlington, the trendsetter of the age and cousin by marriage of Thomas Carter, for whom this Henrietta Street house was built around 1730. Carter was a Master of the Rolls and also related by marriage to Pearce. This is the grandest of all the street's houses and, like Gardiner's number 10, it has been beautifully preserved and occupied by the nuns of the French order of the Daughters of Charity of St. Vincent de Paul, who do so much work for the underprivileged youth of the inner city.

Today, the two nuns' premises (and also their number 8) stand out among the houses in Henrietta Street, which otherwise presents a rather sad shadow of its former self, though efforts are afoot to try to enhance the fabric of what was once one of the finest and broadest red-brick streets in Dublin. It was also one of the first to be developed on a grand scale, with Nathaniel Clements helping Gardiner to complete the street by around the mid-1740s. While off-centre on the city's domestic core, it did show the way

Francis Johnston's choice of a concave screen was a master stroke, as it mitigates the misalignment of Henrietta Street and the King's Inns building. Here, we see the Lord Mayor's coach waiting in front of the entrance to the King's Inns, as an illustration of the type of traffic that was intended to pass along this magnificent street.

for the development of later Georgian complexes in the form of Dublin's squares. Henrietta Street retained its social status and elegance until after the passing of the Act of Union in 1800 — it was recorded in 1792 that the street housed one archbishop, two bishops, four peers and as many members of Parliament.

Pearce was certainly the most famous architect associated with Henrietta Street, and Richard Castle (or Cassells) — his German-born pupil and the man who took over Pearce's practice after his all-too-early death — has, rightly or wrongly, also been suggested as having had an involvement. But it was the most famous of Dublin's architects of the next generation, the English-born James Gandon, who designed the greatest building seen in this drawing,

namely the King's Inns, seen in the upper part of the main picture.

John Rocque's map of Dublin, dating from 1756, shows nothing but fields beyond the top end of Henrietta Street, where the waters of the Royal Canal (seen in the background) were later to flow. It was almost forty years after Rocque that the plan emerged to build the King's Inns there. The centre of the barrister profession had much earlier been located to the south of Christ Church Cathedral, and later it was planned that it should move north of the Liffey to Inns Quay. The question arose as to whether the Society of King's Inns or the Four Courts should occupy the site; the latter's victory enabled Gandon to build another of his great masterpieces, the Four Courts.

The need for the Benchers to seek alternative accommodation gave Gandon a further opportunity to apply his skills to creating a totally different building on fresh ground at the top of Henrietta Street. Other architects had also been asked to submit plans but Gandon's won out, and the foundation stone was laid on August 1st, 1800 — the very day that the disastrous Act of Union got royal assent in London. Gandon's design was U-shaped, with the main front not looking down Henrietta Street — as one might have expected — but away from it, facing some ramshackle buildings on Constitution Hill, which have fortunately since been cleared to allow full view of his façade from the street. The leg of the U (seen on the right of the main image) contains a great hall, Gandon's only unchanged public interior. The Benchers meet here on occasion to dine on 'Commons', an old tradition still preserved and one which budding barristers are obliged to attend. I remember myself, as a student, admiring the bottles of Médoc being warmed in front of the great fireplace, before the Benchers presided over the proceedings from a raised platform at the far end of the room.

Gandon got fed up with the bickering and provocation from the Lord Chancellor and the committee set up to oversee his work, and he offered his resignation around 1808 — a sad end to the career of a man who had shed so much lustre on the nation's capital city. He handed the work on to his able assistant, Henry Aaron Baker, and it was

another important nineteenth-century architect, Francis Johnston, who finally completed the work as Gandon had designed it. The main drawing shows the Inns before wings were added to it in the middle of the nineteenth century.

The link of the two legs of the U was topped by a dome, while the other leg (seen on the left), originally intended to serve as a library, was given over almost exactly two hundred years ago to the Registry of Deeds, which still functions there. A decade later, in 1825–1828, the Benchers demolished what had been the Primate's house at the top of the western side of Henrietta Street and replaced it with Frederick Darley's King's Inns Library, a remarkable and decorative two-storey galleried space where modern technological equipment on the tables seems strangely out of sync with a classical interior decorated in the ancient Greek style.

Francis Johnston, who had taken on the job of completing the Registry of Deeds, also courageously undertook the difficult task of overcoming the awkward change of angle between Henrietta Street and the line of the King's Inns courtyard. This he did by producing a triumphal arch at the top of the street, surmounted by a sculpture of the royal arms. Why the King's Inns was not planned to be the splendid culmination of the walk up Henrietta Street, and in a straight line with it, is a question that remains unsolved — almost an echo of Gardiner's Mall not lining up with the front of the Rotunda Hospital.

SIR EDWARD CARSON, QC

Barristers who trained at the King's Inns included Henry Grattan, Theobald Wolfe Tone, Robert Emmet and

Daniel O'Connell, but crucially, none of them knew the present building. Although Padráig Pearse qualified

as a barrister here in 1901 and was called to the Bar, he only ever defended one case. Instead, as our subject

here, we have Sir Edward Carson, a Dubliner born in Harcourt Street who represents another age and the

tradition of southern unionism. He is seen here as a Queen's Counsel, to which he was appointed in 1889.

Carson famously defended the Marquess of Queensberry in 1895 in the unwise libel case brought by Oscar

Wilde, whose reputation he destroyed. Carson and Wilde had been contemporaries at Trinity College, Dublin;

when Wilde heard that Carson was to take the defence case, he is reported to have said, 'No doubt he will

pursue his case with all the added bitterness of an old friend.' Carson was also the counsel in the real-life case

on which Terence Rattigan's play The Winslow Boy is based.

Edward Carson was elected as a Conservative MP for Dublin University in 1892, and his political career

rose alongside his legal one. He was vehemently opposed to Home Rule for Ireland and helped establish the

Ulster Volunteer Force, the first loyalist paramilitary group. Arms from Germany were available to this force,

just as they were to the planners of the Easter Rising.

Kilmainham features twice in this book, once for the Royal Hospital, and here for the Gaol, both quite close to each other. The two were built more than a century apart and, obviously, for different reasons. The granite gaol was constructed in 1796, at a time when the British government feared an uprising among the Irish. The American colonies had achieved independence only two decades earlier, and the fall of the Bastille in 1789 would have sent shivers down the spine of the British Parliament across the English Channel. It quickly felt the necessity to have a strong prison to incarcerate rebels — if they had not already been shot by British soldiers. As it turned out, government fears were well founded, as the United Irishmen — founded in 1791 and encouraged by Theobald Wolfe Tone — rebelled unsuccessfully in 1798, after which some of their members were executed and others held in the newly built gaol. It was, above all, this event that caused Westminster to pass the Act of Union in 1800, removing the partial independence of Ireland achieved under Grattan's Parliament from 1782 onwards. In 1803 there was another equally unsuccessful revolt. Its leader, Robert Emmet, was hanged and decapitated before his body was buried in Bully's Acre, the cemetery just inside the western wall of the grounds of the Royal Hospital, Kilmainham. It was later recovered by his friends to be buried elsewhere, though no one now knows precisely where.

But for all the role played by nationalistically minded prisoners in the early years of the gaol, its main purpose throughout the nineteenth century was to house non-political criminals, imprisoned for what nowadays we would consider comparatively

The interior of Kilmainham Gaol's east wing, built in 1861, conforms to contemporary thinking about prisoner observation; its horseshoe shape allows fewer wardens to observe more prisoners. This approach may have been based on Jeremy Bentham's ideas from the 1780s, but a completely circular version is seen in Vienna's Narrenturm of 1784, built for serious psychiatric cases also involving incarceration and observation. Kilmainham's Victorian wing is a remarkable space, almost as if a large church has been converted into a prison. In terms of lighting, it was a huge improvement on the conditions in the Georgian west wing, where women prisoners continued to suffer in dark and miserable surroundings. The gaol was empty by 1924 and officially closed in 1929, in spite of the east wing being relatively modern and as serviceable as many other such institutions abroad. Clearly the association with 1916 meant that Irishmen were never to be imprisoned there again; and there was an added rawness in that during the Irish Civil War republican prisoners had been executed in the prison yard by the Free State government.

minor offences. Children as young as eleven were detained and given multiple whippings for crimes such as stealing hay or ropes, or given two months' hard labour for robbing apples from an orchard. Hard times they were, when adults could even be executed for stealing horses.

Before this gaol in Kilmainham was opened – for it had a predecessor on the site – conditions were horrific in Irish prisons. The guards were often cruel, and the atmosphere was generally one of squalor, except for the rich inmates, who could bribe the prison authorities to be allowed have not one but several rooms for themselves, and who were even allowed bring in members of their own family to live with them. For the poor, however, there were no such liberties; small rations of oatmeal, milk, bread and water were their lot, though they were able to get whiskey passed in from outside, which sometimes had them overcome with alcohol even before the midday bell had rung. This was what the English prison reformer John Howard experienced when he visited the old Kilmainham gaol, and

he strove throughout his life to improve the lot of prisoners in gaols on both sides of the Irish Sea. He succeeded in getting a parliamentary Act passed which would provide for better living conditions. He encouraged the siting of prisons on heights in order to improve ventilation, which it was thought would help prevent disease; still, the prisoners spent twenty-three hours a day confined to their cells to encourage thoughts of repentance for their sins, with the aid of bible readings.

The present Kilmainham Gaol was built with these notions in mind, and a visitor to the institution today is starkly reminded of the harsh life in nineteenth-century Irish prisons – dingy passages and small cells bolted on the outside, with but small apertures through which to pass the meagre rations of food. Many a poor prisoner slept with only a little straw to prevent him – or, as was often the case, her – dying of cold from lying on the stones beneath. This happened all too frequently when the prison became overcrowded, and particularly during the disastrous Famine years of 1845–1848, when people would commit crime in order to get into the prison and be fed there instead of dying from starvation outside.

Conditions did improve, at least for some, with the erection of a new east wing in 1861, which is illustrated in the drawing here. It embodied the latest progressive humanitarian thinking on prison life, though seen mainly from a male perspective. The women were never cared for as well as the men, and when the new wing was built, it was reserved for male prisoners; the women were left to their life of solitude in the old, decrepit eighteenth-century cells that the men had vacated. This new wing, designed by John McCurdy – an architect who had recently been working on the more commodious interiors of the Shelbourne Hotel – provided over ninety new cells. All of these faced onto a central open court with a glazed roof, which let in more light and helped the warders keep an eye on every single prisoner. Light also played a role in the cells, as the only window was just under the ceiling, so that the prisoner would look heavenwards when he sought a view. This was the case in the cells on all three floors of this new wing, which nowadays is kept so clean that it has been used for films requiring shots of prison interiors, *The Italian Job*, *In the Name of the Father* and *Michael Collins* being among the notable examples.

Towards the end of the nineteenth century, the gaol again became the home of political prisoners, the most famous of whom was Charles Stewart Parnell. The efforts of this much admired patriot in the Land League to get better working conditions for peasant farmers made him a threat to the government, so he was arrested and incarcerated in Kilmainham in 1881. After lengthy negotiations with the Ireland-friendly British Prime Minister William Ewart Gladstone, Parnell was freed the following year and spent the rest of his life fighting for Home Rule.

But, for modern Ireland, the importance of Kilmainham Gaol centres on its association with the happenings of 1916, the War of Independence and the Civil War. The Rising in Dublin and the reading of the Proclamation of the Irish Republic outside the General Post Office in O'Connell Street in April 1916 led to its signatories being arrested, court-martialled and sentenced to death for their attempt to gain Ireland's freedom from British rule in the midst of World War I. All seven signatories were

AROUND KILMAINHAM GAOL

This part of Dublin holds memories of many different Irish lives over a thousand years. It was the reputed camp of Brian Boru before the Battle of Clontarf in 1014, and according to tradition, the bodies of his slain son Murrough and grandson Turlough were interred near the tenth-century cross in Bully's Acre Cemetery. Army veterans were housed at the Royal Hospital for almost 250 years; participants of the 1916 Rising and the Irish Civil War were imprisoned and executed at the Gaol; and the nearby Irish National War Memorial Gardens are dedicated to the fifty thousand Irish soldiers who died in World War I, many in the fierce fighting of the Somme in 1916.

subsequently brought to Kilmainham Gaol, where they were summarily executed in May 1916 by firing squad, along with seven others. These executions took place in what was the high-walled stonebreaker's yard, a dismally silent place to die. One romantic tale emerged through the poet Joseph Plunkett, who was married to his artist fiancée Grace Gifford in the chapel at midnight and then given ten minutes alone with her before being brought out the following morning to be shot.

These brutal executions, ruthlessly carried out under the authority of the British general John Maxwell to act as an example to others, had the effect of turning many people against the government. The revolutionaries ousted what had been Parnell's old Parliamentary Party in the election of 1918 and set up an independent Parliament or Dáil in January 1919, which adopted a Provisional Constitution and approved a Declaration of Independence. This put the Irish leadership on a collision course with the British government; hated auxiliary troops were brought in to stem the revolt in what became a War of Independence. This ended with a treaty between the British and Irish governments in 1921, which gave virtual independence to twenty-six of the thirty-two counties of the island of Ireland, the other six remaining in union with Britain. Opinions were divided among ordinary Irish people; some were happy to accept the treaty, others violently opposed it, saying that nothing but the independence of the whole island would do. There followed a bloody Civil War, in which many of the anti-treaty activists were imprisoned – and some even shot – in Kilmainham Gaol. The last to leave was Éamon de Valera, inaugurated president of the Republic many years later. After him the prison was closed, to become the largest empty prison in the whole of Europe.

Kilmainham Gaol's tragic history had memories which some kept alive and others preferred to forget. But, in the 1960s, an active group of volunteers got together to prevent the building falling into ruin, restoring it as their limited funds allowed. The chapel, poignant for the marriage of Plunkett and Gifford in 1916, was restored in 1974. Finally, in 1986, the Office of Public Works took over the gaol, and it has since become a major tourist attraction. Its east wing was provided with a new roof in time for the centenary of 1916, when it played such a pivotal role in the country's history. Built four years before the Act of Union and closed down two years after the Anglo-Irish Treaty of 1922, the existence of Kilmainham as an active gaol effectively brackets the period when Irish nationalism strove – at first in vain but in the end successfully – against British rule for most of the country.

THE GEORGIAN
ENTRANCE

The main entrance to the gaol is Georgian. It is approached from the street between curved screens, the one on the right having blind windows that hide an exercise yard. Public executions used to take place in front of the entrance until the early nineteenth century, and this image shows the forbidding — not to say terrifying — carving of chained serpents above the studded door.

RESIDE

DUB

circa 1840

Of Dublin's centre-city squares, Fitzwilliam could be described as one of the latest; building was not started until 1797, and it took just over thirty years to complete. Probably the main reason for the delay was the Act of Union of 1800, which saw many of the prosperous (and often aristocratic) owners of Dublin houses deserting the city and moving to the centre of power and society life in London. But, for all that, the square has remained as intact as its larger and more famous neighbour Merrion Square, and even more so than Stephen's Green, which we may regard as a square though it does not bear the name.

Fitzwilliam Square's integrity and uniform appearance is to be credited to two remarkable families, and one even more remarkable lady. The first family was that of Lord Richard Fitzwilliam, the 7th Viscount, on whose land it was built, and who was also responsible for laying out Merrion Square. When he died in 1816, the estate was taken over by a second family (equally of Norman extraction), that of the Earls of Pembroke, after whom some of the adjoining streets were named. The lady was Barbara Verschoyle, whose father, Bryan Fagan, had been Fitzwilliam's agent. Upon his death, Fagan's wife Elizabeth took over the estate's administration; she, in turn, passed it on to her daughter Barbara, who remained agent for forty years until she died in 1835. She had a great relationship with the 7th Viscount, to whom she was much attached. As an ardent Catholic, she probably did not try to convert him from his Protestant faith, but she did so to her husband, Richard Verschoyle, with whom she was involved in many charitable causes. It can't have been easy for her to keep up the momentum;

KEY TO FITZWILLIAM SQUARE SOUTH

TOWN GARDENS ARE SOMETIMES DETAILED ON LARGE-SCALE ORDNANCE SURVEY MAPS

NUMBER 36: THE ARTIST MAINIE JELLETT LIVED HERE

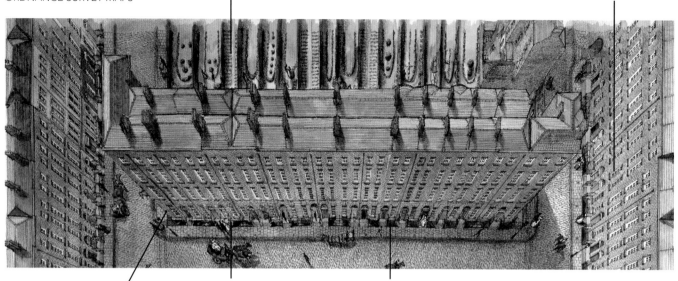

NUMBER 18: HOUSE ASSOCIATED WITH JACK B. YEATS

NUMBER 21: THE HOUSE OF ELIZABETH, LADY BRANDEN

NUMBERS 24–35 HAVE RUSTICATED STONE GROUND FLOOR LEVELS, STONE CORNICES AND, IN SOME CASES, QUOINS (MASONRY BLOCKS AT THE CORNER OF A WALL OR BETWEEN HOUSES). THESE WERE REFINEMENTS ADDED BY THE BUILDER

leases that demanded buildings be erected within a short number of years were often quietly ignored for twenty or thirty years, and plots lay empty for decades. The west side of the square, that with the most traffic nowadays, was the first to be built in its entirety, followed by the east and south side by the 1820s, but it took the whole thirty-year span for the north side ('the sunny side of the street') to be completed.

Unlike in Stephen's Green, where there was many an aristocratic owner, the effect of the Act of Union was to bring the owners of the Fitzwilliam Square houses slightly lower down the social scale. In the words of Maria Edgeworth in her novel *The Absentee*, 'In Dublin, commerce rose into the vacated seats of rank; wealth rose into the place of birth.' The upper echelons in Fitzwilliam Square were professional men — lawyers, doctors, bankers, architects and engineers — but there were also many from the commercial world, including tradespeople and carpenters. Their leases laid down strict conditions as to height, which, of course, led to the uniform appearance of the houses. These were to be of red brick, not showy; no bow windows, for instance. Their only embellishment would be the doorways of different architectural orders, including that feature so typical of Georgian Dublin, the semi-circular fanlight above the door, of which so many fortunately survive. A little show is provided by the railings flanking the few steps up to the door, put up to prevent passers-by from falling into the basement. Differing shades of brick give a certain amount of visual variety, and the recessed windows (often decreasing in size as their floors rise) bring out the orderly rhythm of the houses, particularly in the evening sun.

In comparison to those in Merrion Square, the Fitzwilliam Square houses tend to be narrower and, while they lack on the whole the riotous stucco ornament of the earlier and more important houses in the city, there still survive a number of decorative interiors – best seen on a walk around the square on a winter evening, when the internal lighting helps to bring out the fine ceilings of the ground and first floors. Most of the windows retain their original twelve-pane division, and those that no longer do so tend to stick out like sore thumbs! Inside the houses, one attractive, old-fashioned characteristic is the presence of shutters, which were usual at the time but are nowadays all too often replaced by curtains. An unusual element among the furnishings of some of the houses is a waist-high brass rail attached to the hall wall just inside the door – a feature which has puzzled many in search of a rational explanation.

KEY TO FITZWILLIAM SQUARE EAST

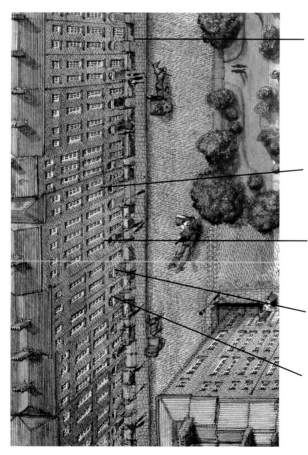

NUMBER 10: ONE OF THE FEW HOUSES ALL OF WHOSE ORIGINAL EXTERIOR FEATURES HAVE SURVIVED TO THIS DAY

NUMBER 5: AN EXCEPTIONALLY NARROW HOUSE

NUMBER 3: THIS HOUSE RETAINS MANY ORIGINAL FEATURES. A NINETEENTH-CENTURY ORNAMENTAL WATER TANK CAN BE SEEN IN ITS BASEMENT AREA

NUMBER 2: THE FORMER HOME OF WILLIAM DARGAN

NUMBER 1: THE RESIDENCE OF THE HONE FAMILY, INCLUDING ARTIST EVIE

DUBLIN'S SQUARES

Fitzwilliam is the smallest of Dublin's central Georgian squares, but it has stayed closest to its original form and function. St. Stephen's Green, walled in by the Corporation in the seventeenth century, is the largest and oldest of such spaces in the city. Its walls gave way to railings in the early nineteenth century, when the space came into the ownership of local residents, who had exclusive access to it until 1877; from 1880 it was open to all, having been restyled in the Victorian manner. Next largest was Merrion Square, originally laid out in 1762 and accessible only to residents until the 1960s; it has three main lawns, connected by curving paths, and other areas of naturalistic planting, now open to all. Mountjoy Square is a true square shape and dates from the 1790s, being part of the later developments by the Gardiner family. Half of it retains its early nineteenth-century formal layout, while the other half consists of sports facilities, open to the public. Parnell (formerly Rutland) Square had walled gardens as part of Dr. Mosse's pleasure gardens (see pp.98–99 and following for the history of the site). Fitzwilliam Square is the last example of a Dublin city square with access only by key.

The professional classes who were among the first inhabitants of Fitzwilliam Square have managed to retain their presence, so the buildings are well looked after. During the first half of the last century, many of the houses were used as offices or consulting rooms, particularly for the medical doctors who proliferated in the square. But private families (for whom the houses were originally built) are slowly beginning to occupy individual houses again for themselves.

For such a beautiful area, it is not surprising that the square accommodated a number of famous people in its day. William Dargan, to whom we owe the construction of so many of our railways, lived in number 2. Number 3 was the home of Lady Elizabeth Branden (née La Touche), who held here a famous salon. One of its most frequent visitors was William Lamb, the Chief Secretary, who, as Lord Melbourne, would later become Queen Victoria's first prime minister. Lord Branden took proceedings against Melbourne, accusing him of 'criminal conversation' with his wife, but the case was subsequently dropped, perhaps for 'a consideration'. The poet W.B. Yeats moved to number 42 from his Merrion Square quarters, and his brother, the artist Jack B., had his studio in the enlarged house on the corner with Fitzwilliam Place. Other artists who spent part of their lives in the square included William Orpen, Evie Hone, Rose Barton and Mainie Jellett. Mainie's sister Bay sat knitting in a deckchair outside her house at number 36 while the Corporation workmen tried in vain to remove the granite flags on the pavement outside her house, which is why they still remain there.

In addition to the beauty and uniformity of the square's buildings, so much admired by those in modern tour buses, the magic of Fitzwilliam Square is provided by the garden in the centre. Unlike other square-gardens in the city, which are open to the public, this one is railed off and accessible only to those who have a key, mainly people who own or rent houses on the square. The garden was created in 1813, even before many of the east- and south-side houses had been built. The Act instituting the 'inclosing, lighting and improving' of the garden initiated the setting up of a commission of fourteen owners or residents to govern and maintain it. Subsequently, dogs, bows and arrows, football, archery and even croquet were forbidden; 'cricket, hockey and all such rough games' were also banned. The only sport allowed was tennis, and the Irish Lawn Tennis Championships were held in the garden in the 1890s, when six courts were neatly fitted in to the space available. These tests of sporting prowess became social events with bands playing — there were even ballads specially composed by Percy French.

When the 150-year lease expired in 1963, the fourteen commissioners of the time had to be disbanded, and the gardens became neglected. By 1971, however, the Earl of Pembroke leased the garden to the Fitzwilliam Square Association, which continues the task of keeping the garden to the design of the original layout of more than two hundred years ago.

A GEORGIAN HOUSE DISSECTED

Properties varied considerably according to their use and the owner's family circumstances. This house is on the substantial side; it probably belongs to a higher government official.

A nurse — today a nanny — would have cared for the children if the parents were expected to socialise regularly. There would have been many other servants, some seen above stairs and others confined to outside, including a coachman. Stable mews survive behind some of the houses of Fitzwilliam Square and are constructed from a variety of materials, including brick and stone.

Sadly many such properties were put to the test as tenements in north Dublin city from the nineteenth century until the mid-twentieth century. Conditions for the people crowded into them were appalling, and the houses fared badly; whole streets were eventually lost, for example Summerhill, demolished in 1981.

TOP FLOOR: Occupied by children and servants, it could be reached by a boxed-in staircase. The nursery may be on this level, where the ceilings would be much lower.

SECOND FLOOR: Depending on the depth of the house, there could be two good-sized bedrooms here, possibly with a dressing room each. Washing would be in a portable bath, which the servants would fill. Chamber pots were the order of the day when Fitzwilliam Square was built, concealed in a pot-stand before and after use.

FIRST FLOOR: At the front, a grand drawing room for entertaining, with either another reception room or a bedroom at the rear. Many houses had double doors that retreated into wall pockets between the rooms, thereby transforming the space for circulation when company was expected. The windows are at their tallest on this floor.

GROUND FLOOR: Some entrance hallways are impressive rooms in themselves, most notably on Merrion Square and St. Stephen's Green. The adjoining room at the front may be a parlour, and behind there is a room used for dining. Many of Dublin's houses feature beautiful doorways with columns and fanlights above, as seen here.

BASEMENT: Storage vaults for coal and wood are under the pavement – Fitzwilliam Square has some fine survivals of cast-iron coalhole covers set into granite flags. Cooking is carried out in the kitchen at the front of the house, while the rooms at the back function as a servant's hall and eating room. Storage vaults may be found here. There may be an outside privy in the garden area, which has to be dug out and emptied periodically.

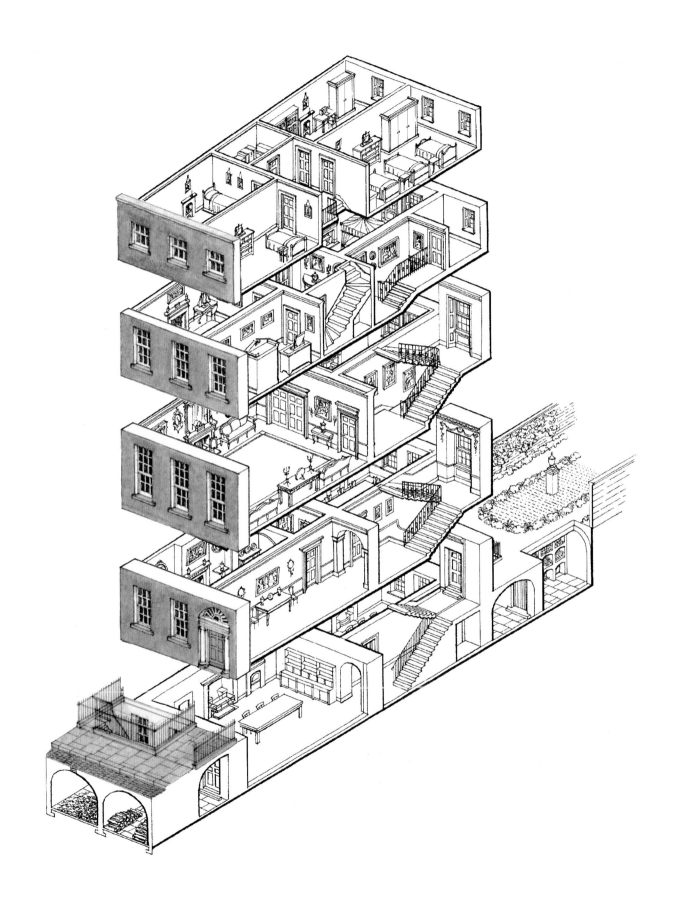

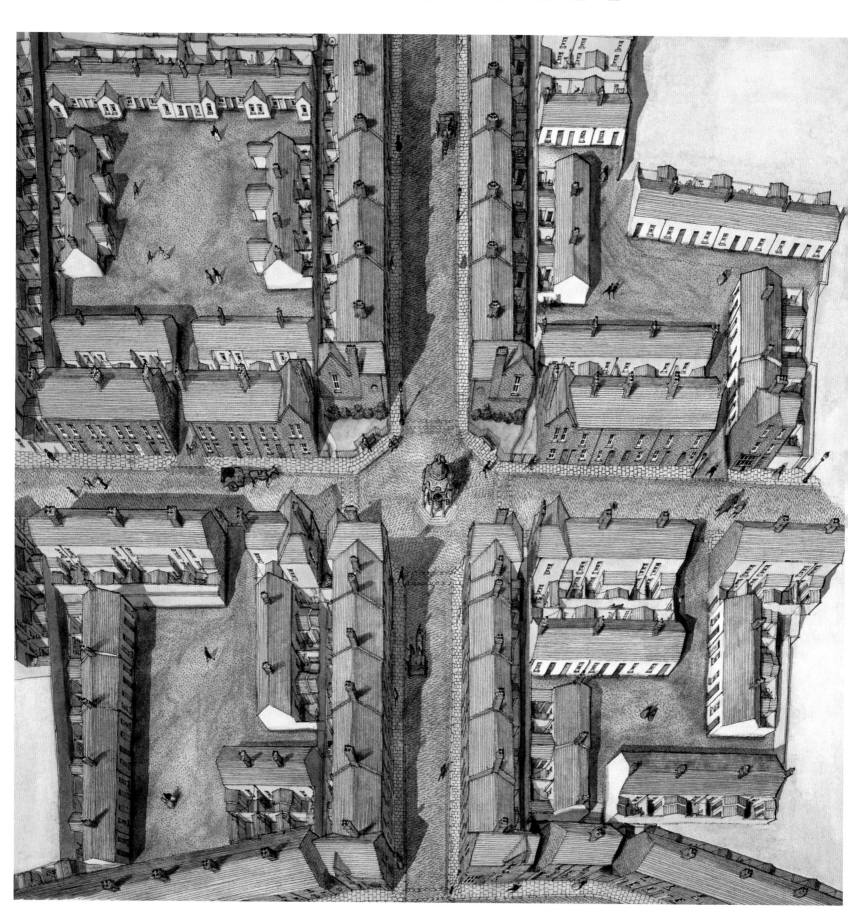

circa 1900

The Liberties is an area west of St. Patrick's Cathedral, including the Coombe, which many would see as the part of the city where the real 'Dubs' come from. The word 'Liberties' has medieval origins; the first Liberty, established on lands close to St. Patrick's Cathedral in the thirteenth century, had its own courts which could give legal judgments independent of civic courts or of the city fathers. By the time of the Reformation, the number of Liberties had increased. The richest of them was that of Donore, owned by the Vice-Treasurer William Brabazon, who created it out of lands earlier owned by St. Mary's Abbey. Separate fairs were organised in the seventeenth century, and the arrival of Protestant Dutch traders and tradesmen meant that the Liberties gradually became an established centre for craftsmanship, aided by a plentiful supply of water for 'dirt' industries such as tanning. Some of these occupations were also carried on by native Catholics, who must have made up almost half of the Liberties' population. Relations between the two religions occasionally flared up into conflict, which was, however, usually short-lived. Both the population and the economy of the Liberties went up and down like a see-saw, but the predominant impression created throughout the late-eighteenth and the first three-quarters of the nineteenth century was one of abject and unrelieved poverty, with anything up to four families living in a single room; in 1798, it was recorded that the average number of tenants in any one house was almost thirty. If, as occasionally happened, the water became contaminated, the danger of cholera, dysentery and typhus raised its ugly head to stalk the population.

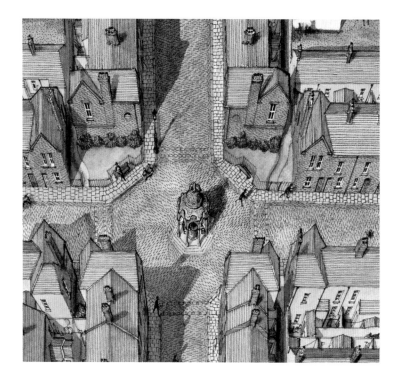

AT THE CROSSROADS

The central crossing of this development includes larger brick houses that feature small, circular windows looking in towards the drinking fountain. These houses have windows on three sides, and their detailing includes brick cornices and friezes. There was also a water trough for horses, not visible here. At the foot of the main picture is the street called The Coombe, on which the Weavers' Hall stood until demolished in 1956. The hall was built with a loan from David Digges La Touche (1671–1745). His grandson Peter La Touche, a partner in the family bank, bought a house on Fitzwilliam Square for his daughter Elizabeth, later Lady Branden (see p. 152).

Marie-Anne de Bovet, a French lady who visited the Liberties in the second half of the nineteenth century, was very critical of the living conditions – 'tumbledown mouldy-looking houses, reeking of dirt, and oozing with the disgusting smell of accumulated filth of many generations' – and described the shops offering 'sides of rancid bacon, bundles of candles, and jars of treacle – a delicacy as much sought after as soap is neglected'. Shoes taken out of pawn on a Saturday night in preparation for Sunday Mass were pledged again on Monday morning. But 'all of these ragged and vermin-covered people are most affable', de Bovet continued, 'and it touches one to see the good-temper, sociableness and even politeness that survive such degradation'.

The industrial focus of the Liberties was on wool prod-ucts and weaving, and there are tragic tales of respectable weavers becoming so poor that they had to demean themselves by going out begging. More fortunate was Jonathan Fisher, who started out as a 'woollen-draper' in the Liberties and became one of the best-known Irish landscape painters of the eighteenth century. He was only a few years younger than an even more famous Liberties artist in the shape of George Barret.

In the last quarter of the nineteenth century, it seemed as if salvation was at hand for the poverty-stricken inhabitants of the Liberties. Because sanitation was desperately in need of improvement, a Dublin Sanitary Association was set up, which, in turn, spawned the creation of the Dublin Artisans Dwellings Company, founded in 1876. The Association had instigated that the 1875 English

Artisans' and Labourers' Dwellings Improvement Act be extended to Ireland, and this gave local authorities the opportunity to sweep away slums with the aid of government loans. The areas thus cleared could then be sold to builders for the construction of improved working-class housing. At one fell swoop, many of the old buildings of the Liberties were demolished, including some fine old structures, but most of them were just tenements housing the poorest of the poor.

The Artisans Dwelling Company was a privately owned firm and the most effective body in the city providing houses for the working classes, of which they built 3,300 before they ceased construction around 1908. Its most imaginative scheme was completed in the 1880s in the Liberties, as seen here in the drawing. Consisting of two

hundred houses on four acres, it formed what was almost a square, divided cross-like into four quarters, with Gray Street and Reginald Street crossing each other in the centre. The houses were in two-storey rows, with taller gables and small round windows marking out the larger houses at the crossing. Furthermore, each of the corners created by the street pattern had a series of charming cottages in behind the rows of two-storey houses, forming a square within a square, some bearing the name of the family that still owned the land – the Brabazons, Earls of Meath. This was Victorian town planning of high quality, which it is a pleasure to walk through today. The buzz of motorised traffic seems far away at the centre, marked by a shamrock-decorated, eight-pillared Victorian canopy (replaced after the original was demolished by an errant

BRABAZON SQUARE

Looking at maps from before the area was rebuilt, we see that this part of the site was enclosed by Cole Alley, Elbow Lane and Pimlico. Narrow lanes with further entries off them were perfect for slum landlords. After rebuilding, as we see here, white-washed, single-storey houses replaced the tenement buildings. The neat, new houses are similar to those seen in other parts of the city, as the Artisans Dwelling Company was active in several areas of south Dublin, including Harold's Cross. Brabazon was a family name of the Earls of Meath.

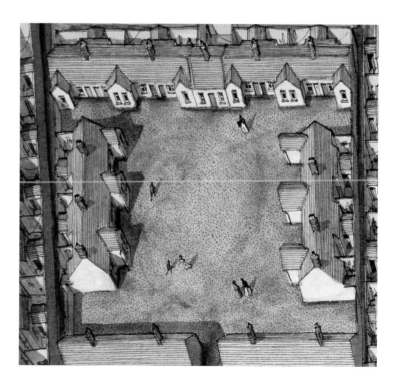

lorry). It houses a statue of the Sacred Heart to commemorate the centenary of Catholic Emancipation, but the display was re-modelled half a century later to mark the visit to the Liberties of Pope John Paul II in 1979.

The peace and quiet engendered by this lovely oasis bring us back to its foundation more than a century and a quarter ago, and this area, more than most others in the city, has changed little since its creation. But such placid beauty was of little value to the original inhabitants of the Liberties, who had been uprooted from their old, squalid homes to give way to these new smart and tidy houses. The rents charged by the Artisans Dwelling Company were so high that they could be paid only by those artisans who were earning sufficient wages, but that was more than the old inhabitants were able to afford. In the end, there was not a single person from the old Liberties population who occupied any of the new, fancy dwellings. Five hundred families had to leave the old, familiar haunts where they had grown up and migrate in towards the centre of the city, where they swelled the numbers in the already overcrowded tenements which persisted well into the second half of the twentieth century. But the modern artisans of the Liberties still retain the good humour and repartee of their predecessors so praised by that French lady who visited the area a century and a half ago.

THE DRINKING FOUNTAIN
IN GRAY STREET

The Glasgow firm of Walter Macfarlane & Co. operated between 1850 and 1965, and supplied its cast iron to many countries under the name of the Saracen Foundry. The adjective 'saracenic' could certainly be applied to the style of their elaborate kiosk–like structures with filigree work, seen as being 'Moorish'. Their designs included bandstands and drinking fountains, and even the canopy of the Olympia Theatre in Dublin. These products could be ordered from a catalogue, with different decorative motifs to be chosen and inserted as desired.

The fountain in Gray Street dated from 1884 and is seen here in its original glory. According to a report, it lost its eagle in action by the Black and Tans and was converted into a shrine to the Sacred Heart in 1929. In the 1970s, it was badly damaged by a lorry. A substitute roof is in position today, so little of the original remains.

A similar fountain is to be found in Dún Laoghaire. It has a large crown on the top, commemorating a visit by Queen Victoria in 1900. After being seriously damaged in a 1981 attack, it has since been restored to working order, with its original colour scheme recreated.

POST-EMAN

CHU

BUIL

BUIL

ST. PAUL'S

1837 building; 1980s surroundings

When going up or down the Dublin Quays today, it is difficult to realise that up to little more than three hundred years ago, there would have been largely just a tidal marsh and green fields going down to the river's edge, with boats drawn up on the shore. One would have expected the Quays to have been built by the Dublin Corporation, but no: surprisingly, it was ambitious developers who undertook the enormous task. On the north side, it was Humphrey Jervis (whose name lives on in Jervis Street and the Luas stop there) who did the job below the Four Courts, and William Ellis who did it upstream. It was the latter who, in 1692, built Arran Quay, named after Richard Butler, Earl of Arran and deputy Lord Lieutenant to his father, the famous Duke of Ormonde. There was one gap further upstream which remained unfilled until 1811, after which the Quays could be said to have been completed.

It was facing onto Arran Quay that St. Paul's Church was built in the 1830s. Before that, Catholic churches in the city, though often well appointed inside, did not purposely draw any attention to themselves on the outside, and were placed off main streets. St. Teresa's Church on Clarendon Street, off Grafton Street (built 1793–1810), is a well-known example. One commentator, William Meagher, reflecting on the past in 1853, described these 'back-street' churches as 'crouching timidly in the darkest and most loathsome alleys and lanes of the city' – all of this because, throughout most of the eighteenth century, the Catholics of the city were considerably disadvantaged in practising their religion. Things began to change with the passing of a Catholic

The issue of extended towers on churches is an interesting one. Similar structures in classical times were no taller than one or two stages, and most functioned as lanterns to light an interior space below. The need for them developed along with Christianity's desire to ring bells. Renaissance architects had to design tall and sturdy structures that could be both seen and heard. Patrick Byrne's church shows considerable restraint when compared with St. George's of Hardwicke Place, by Francis Johnston, which keeps going for another three levels, the last being a stone spire.

Relief Act in 1793 which deemed that former 'restraints and disabilities shall be discontinued'. While St. Teresa's in Clarendon Street was not completed until 1810, it was the building of the Pro-Cathedral on Marlborough Street (1814–1825) that trumpeted a trend for Dublin churches to come out of their hiding places onto more visible locations. Our Lady of Mount Carmel on Whitefriar Street continued the process on the south side in the late 1820s. Daniel O'Connell's achievement of getting the Westminster Parliament to pass the Act of Catholic Emancipation in 1829 gave Catholics their longed-for freedom; it also led to a spate of churches following the classical model of the Pro-Cathedral in featuring a pillared portico in front, such as in St. Andrew's in Westland Row (1832–1834, but only completed in 1843) and Adam & Eve's on Merchant's Quay, almost opposite St. Paul's. These forerunners inspired Canon (later Monsignor) Yore, parish priest of St. Paul's, to acquire a narrow site on Arran Quay, where he built his church in full view of everyone walking and coaching up and down the Quays, with the best view to be seen from the south side.

Virtually the whole width of the church is taken up by

the granite Ionic portico, its capitals outstandingly well carved for such a hard material and featuring on their collars the Greek anthemion or honeysuckle, imitated from the designs of the Erectheum on the Athenian Acropolis. The church stands out even more because of its two-tier domed tower (also featuring the honeysuckle motif), which is even taller than the portico itself. It bears a large clock on each face and has a peal of bells occasionally tolled by Martin, the caretaker. The pinnacle of the portico has a statue of St. Paul by Constantine Panormo, flanked by St. Peter and St. Patrick by J.R. Kirk. The narrowness of the site and the height of the tower make St. Paul's look very tall and thin when seen from a distance.

St. Paul's was designed by Patrick Byrne, the subject of a detailed biography by Brendan Grimes, *Majestic Shrines and Graceful Sanctuaries* (2009). In it, we learn to our surprise that the architect was already fifty-two when he started on this, his first church, having probably busied himself with building houses in earlier years. That activity must have provided him with sufficient credentials for Canon Yore to give him the contract, and later in his career he built many churches in Dublin and elsewhere over a period of thirty years. He started here with the neo-classical – and particularly Greek – style, in later years adopting the neo-Gothic being propagated by Augustus Welby Pugin, before returning towards the end of his life to his original neo-classical mode.

IMMEDIATE NEIGHBOURS

These houses are shown in the late 1980s and have since been demolished. The site is now occupied by a terrace of neo-Georgian-style houses, all five-storeyed. The replacements have equal-sized windows on the three inner floors, making them less convincing, but they are part of an attempt to make new housing fit the location. Some eighty-five metres behind them runs Hammond Lane, at one stage the likely shoreline of the River Liffey.

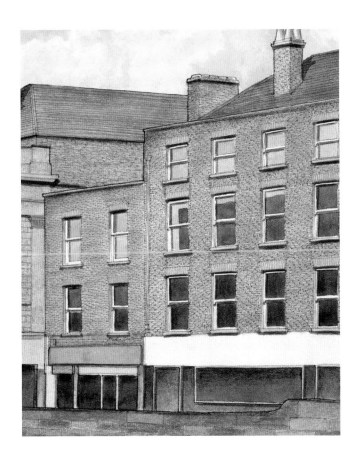

Byrne certainly made his mark with St. Paul's, one of the most striking Catholic churches on the north side of the Liffey after the Pro-Cathedral of two decades earlier. In contrast to its somewhat cold granite frontage, the oblong interior of St. Paul's is now warmly coloured (after it had fallen into disuse for a considerable time). It has a shallow, barrel-vaulted ceiling of five separate compartments, each decorated with rosettes, matching the full-height pilasters in between the large windows on the upper half of the walls. The honeysuckle motif appears again on the Ionic capitals of the pair of pillars approaching the apse, the space between them letting us view the clever lighting coming in from above on the vertical wall of the apse, which bears a large, curved canvas by F.S. Barff depicting the conversion of St. Paul on the road to Damascus. In 1862, it replaced a crucifixion, based on that of a London church which had a similarly striking lighting style in the apse, and which must have sufficiently impressed the middle-aged Irish architect to repeat the scheme on his first church here on Arran Quay.

It took only two years to open the church to the public but another five to finish the portico, into which most of the money fundraised from various religious denominations went, at a time when financial contributions were matching rising church attendances. In comparison to its predecessor of 1730 — reconstructed in 1785–1786 — which was further away from the Quay, the new St. Paul's was to parade the Catholic faith before the public, giving support and confidence to the city's Catholic population, who had been downtrodden for the previous two centuries. Churches such as St. Paul's were seen to provide an advantageous influence on the morals of the parishioners, giving them the right to be seen as equals of the Protestants — whose steeples they were often seen to be out-trumping in height during the remainder of the nineteenth century — and, as Brendan Grimes put it, 'to command respect from all levels of society'.

In recent years, the local parishioners have dwindled somewhat, probably because many moved out to the suburbs. The Diocese of Dublin has given the church over to the Evangelical Movement, which allows a Taizé mass to be celebrated on Saturday evenings. On Sundays, St. Paul's hosts an ethnic Christian community who happily take advantage of the facilities offered to them to worship according to their own particular rite.

A CLOSER LOOK AT ST. PAUL'S

St. Paul's gives a pleasing impression from across the river and was built in scale with its surroundings. At close quarters, the design and execution of the exterior are equally impressive.
The granite has weathered extremely well, and the quality of its carving will no doubt outlast many
structures of more recent years.

The cornice — the level projecting furthest out from the building near the top of this
image — is recessed underneath, as was that of the Erectheum in Athens. The objection to
Christian churches being built in a classical style was that prototypes such as the Erectheum,
a shrine dedicated to a legendary Greek hero, were heathen. This classical original upon which the
building's crisp details were based would have been painted, with its mouldings and decoration highly
coloured. Any severity in the stone finish is dispelled by the flattering light of a summer's evening.

THE CHURCH OF
ST. AUGUSTINE & ST. JOHN

1860 building; 1980s surroundings

The Augustinian friars established themselves in Dublin as early as the second half of the thirteenth century but, a hundred or so years on, tensions arose between the Irish and the English friars in the community, which led to the murder of one of them – probably an 'inside job'! At the same time, the friars were chaplains to Dublin Castle, which is understandable because their church – on what is now Thomas Street, just outside the New (or western) Gate into the city – was only a few hundred yards away from the castle. One of their number was even briefly an archbishop of Dublin. But with the Reformation and Henry VIII's suppression of the monasteries, the friary's buildings and lands were taken by the king, and for more than three centuries the friars led a secretive life and were not allowed to practise their religion openly. In the meantime, the property that was once theirs served Sir William Petty in the mid-seventeenth century as headquarters for his famous Down Survey, the first general mapping of the whole country. It later became the site of a very successful music hall. All the while, the twenty-four-metre-high tower of St. Magdalene's Chapel, which formed part of a hospital on the site associated with the Augustinians, remained standing until demolished around 1800, but not before Gabriel Beranger was able to sketch it around 1780. This was the last visual remnant of the old medieval Augustinian foundation which stood almost exactly where the belfry of the present Church of St. Augustine & St. John, known as John's Lane Church, now stands in Thomas Street.

Sometime around 1700, the friars were able to acquire a warehouse for Masses in

The Church of St. Augustine & St. John's tower, by contrast with that of St. Paul's on Arran Quay, comes from the canon of 'Christian' building styles, so its tower is a traditional feature for Edward Welby Pugin to have added above this, the apparent west end of the church. The tower is rectangular in plan, with one arched window to each side and two when the church is viewed face-on.

John's Lane, off Thomas Street, which was replaced in 1746 by a larger structure, eighteen metres by seven, which — surprisingly for a Catholic chapel at the time — had columns, a gilded tabernacle and a painting of the crucifixion as an altarpiece. It was extended in 1781. But the present church is on a different site, that of the old medieval friary, and was on land bought from the well-known heart surgeon Dominic Corrigan. The foundation stone for the new structure was laid by Dublin's archbishop, Cardinal Cullen, in 1862, to the accompaniment of a grand sermon and music by Mozart and Weber, but it took over thirty years for the church to be completed. The steeple and roof of the nave were finished by 1874, when the church first opened for public worship. Much fundraising was needed before the apse could be finished in 1895, allowing for the full church to be finally consecrated.

The architect chosen for the initial design was Edward Welby Pugin, son of the more famous Augustus Welby Pugin, and he produced what is undoubtedly one of the most decorous nineteenth-century churches in the city. Pugin did not live to see the completion of his masterpiece, but the work continued under his former partner, George Ashlin, and it was William Hague who was responsible for adding the apse. The church's steeple is outstanding in every sense: sixty-eight metres high, with a great peal of bells, rectangular in plan and dominating the whole area — including the Liberties nearby, from which John's Lane Church has traditionally drawn many of its parishioners. It carries the decorative interplay of layers of grey granite and bright-red sandstone (extensively con-

served in 1987–1991), which, together, characterise the whole exterior, including the long sides, one of which is particularly well viewed from John's Street. The lower half of the steeple presents a very tall, pointed arch with a richly traceried window, beneath which is the entrance, under a pointed hood. At the centre is a figure of Christ (1873) surrounded by a veritable orchestra of angels playing their various instruments — reminiscent of the joyful musicians on the Pórtico de la Gloria in the Cathedral of Santiago de Compostela — and angels also feature prominently in the arch surrounds.

This leads us into the interior, which Christine Casey's splendid *Dublin* volume of *The Buildings of Ireland* series says is more suggestive of a minor cathedral than a parish

IN LINE WITH THE CHURCH

Many of the surrounding buildings date from the later Georgian period and are of the scale of the three houses shown here, depicted as they were in the late 1980s. The two outer ones still stand today, but the middle one has been replaced in modern red-brick, which at least respects the building line of this important thoroughfare of Thomas Street. To the sides and rear of the church are two streets that bear its name – John's Lane, John Street – as they did in the late eighteenth century, before such a substantial Catholic church building would have been tolerated. It is popularly called the John's Lane Church, possibly a memory from a time when worshippers had to hide their faith in the side streets.

church, even if it is less spectacular than the striking Gothic exterior. The style within is early English, with columns of Cork marble supporting pointed arches, between which project more angels, this time giving rise to the decorative ribs of the ceiling. The apse, the last part of the church to have been completed, has five sides with delicately panelled walls and large windows filled with bright stained glass. These are all by Mayer of Munich, who supplied their religious products to so many Irish churches in the nineteenth century, but with one exception: that on the extreme left, which bears a particular kind of interlace that has recently been identified as a product of the Harry Clarke Studios. Mayer were also responsible for the figures in the large west (though really south) window above the entrance, and in the side chapels forming part of the apse. But the most striking window is that in the wall on the right as you enter, roughly where a transept was originally planned but never built. It is by Michael Healy, from 1934, and, though somewhat dark, it has wonderfully coloured glass depicting events in the life of St. Augustine. Beside it and opposite, we find other products of the Harry Clarke Studios. Not to be forgotten in the unusually rich decoration of this delightful church are the mosaics — particularly in the lady chapel — and the white spiky marble reredos in the apse, featuring the Holy Family and the baptism of Christ in masterly work by Edmund Sharp, who also created the altar in front of it, with the Last Supper facing the congregation.

The Church of St. Augustine & St. John, so impressive both within and without, is a testimony to the centuries of service which the Augustinian friars have devoted to the citizens of Dublin outside the western walls. This stretched from the medieval period, through the post-Reformation doldrums, up to the more triumphal times of the nineteenth century when — after world-wide fundraising efforts — the friars amassed sufficient funds to build this Victorian gem, which proudly shows its face directly onto Thomas Street, unlike its eighteenth-century predecessor, which had to hide behind where it now stands. In paying tribute to the friars down the centuries, one may pick out a single example in the history of Dublin — Fr. F.X. Martin, O.S.A., whose funeral mass took place here, and who was so prominent in the campaign to save Viking Dublin at Wood Quay, only a few hundred yards away from this Thomas Street church.

A CARVING OF AN ANGEL-MUSICIAN

The angels playing music under the pointed hood of the church's exterior also have their counterparts inside. This is one of several such figures on corbels. In this case the angel is playing a type of dulcimer, and clearly quite rapturously. Other features of the interior, such as the confessionals, are well designed and finished to a high standard. There can be no doubt that Edward Welby Pugin and his craftsmen and artists were aiming to recapture the spirit of Gothic buildings in a very sincere way. Figures such as this one would have been based on surviving carved examples or depictions in manuscripts.

There were plenty of influential figures who favoured the classical style for new churches, among them Cardinal Newman, founder of the Catholic University of Ireland, of which University College, Dublin, is a successor. St. Paul's on Arran Quay and this church are useful examples of how the question of style could be approached in nineteenth-century Ireland. In the latter half of the century, a profusion of styles was used for all kinds of buildings, and by that time builders of churches could be attracted to more than just the neo-classical or neo-Gothic camps. The University Church on St. Stephen's Green is entered by through a neo-Romanesque porch that leads into a neo-Byzantine interior, evoking the atmosphere of Constantinople.

A NEW, INI

IREL

EPENDENT

AND

O'CONNELL STREET

The Dublin of even seventy years ago was a far cry from what it is today; some things have changed utterly, though others remain more or less the same. Take O'Connell Street, for example. It started its life as a mall, built in the eighteenth century by a landowner and speculator named Luke Gardiner, and of it only part of one house remains. For his own good reasons, Gardiner decided not to have the northern end of his street terminate with the front of the recently built Rotunda Hospital, but rather with the gardens adjoining it. The southern end did not reach the River Liffey at the time; this was achieved in the 1790s, at which stage Carlisle (now O'Connell) Bridge was built to connect it with the core of the Georgian city south of the river. But it was largely thanks to the Wide Streets Commission (which had been set up in 1757 and counted Gardiner among its number) that it achieved its present breadth, making it the widest and grandest street in the city. Their foresight — and power to knock down rows of houses to broaden streets — has been a godsend for the city planners of today.

The thoroughfare – formerly Sackville Street and not officially renamed O'Connell Street until 1924 – got its first vertical emphasis in 1808 with a pillar erected to the memory of the admirable Horatio Nelson, victor of the Battle of Trafalgar three years earlier, as seen in the drawing opposite. Placed upon a classical Doric column of granite sitting on a broad, square base, it bore the statue of the admiral carved by Thomas Kirk. Though the column avoided the shelling meted out to neighbouring buildings by a royal naval gunboat during the Easter Rising of 1916, it succumbed to an IRA

GARDINER'S MALL EXTENDED

When Gardiner's Mall, also called Sackville Mall, was built in the eighteenth century, it had the same width as the present-day O'Connell Street but started north of Henry Street and Earl Street and ran to the corner with the Rotunda Hospital. This was on the same alignment as the earlier, and much narrower, Drogheda Street. As intended, the mall became a place of 'polite resort', where people of leisure could promenade. With the opening of Lower Sackville Street after 1790 and the building of Carlisle Bridge (1794) on the site of the present O'Connell Bridge, the world had moved on, and the street became Dublin's principal thoroughfare.

bomb in 1966. What was left of it was destroyed and ultimately replaced by a stainless steel needle in 2001–2003, now known as the Spire.

The target of the gunboat *Helga*'s shelling was the General Post Office, built in the years 1814–1818 and designed by Francis Johnston, who had already distinguished himself through his design for the Gothic chapel in Dublin Castle and the re-organisation of the old Parliament Building into the Bank of Ireland headquarters. For the GPO, as it is generally known to Dubliners, Johnston chose the more decorative Ionic order – in contrast to the simpler Doric of Nelson's Pillar – to ornament a six-columned portico which projects out onto the footpath. This portico and the flanking granite walls fronting onto O'Connell Street are

the only parts of the original GPO to survive; the remainder was gutted in the bombardment of April 1916 after the insurgents made it their headquarters, having read aloud for the first time the Proclamation of the Irish Republic in front of the building. The rebel leaders paid with their lives by being executed the following month, and their heroism is commemorated every Easter Monday by an army march-past and parade, with the Irish President usually taking the salute. The momentous happenings of a century ago are also honoured by the presence of a tricolour flying over the building, seen above at the centre of our picture.

The events of 1916 necessitated the rebuilding of most of the street, after so many of its houses and shops were left in ruins. Those lying north of the GPO, in what is now Upper

O'Connell Street, were reconstructed under the supervision and control of the city architect, who insisted on the new structures retaining a uniform height, while giving a certain freedom in design and fabric used. More scope was allowed in Lower O'Connell Street, seen on the left of the main image, where Eason's, the newsagents, stands out through the presence of the semi-circular tympanum above its entrance and the attic roof rising above the rest.

Fortunately, most of the monuments in O'Connell Street were left intact after 1916. Most notable today is that to Daniel O'Connell, who had gained Emancipation for Irish Catholics in 1829 and after whom the street is called. The statue of 'the Liberator' stands on a rounded pedestal designed by John Henry Foley, who did not live to see its completion. Beneath him are bronze figures representing Patriotism, Courage, Eloquence and Fidelity — all of which O'Connell had in plenty — but their pride was dented by a few bullet holes some decades ago. O'Connell is matched at the other end of the street by Charles Stewart Parnell (see p.186). Other statues of a smaller scale seen here are those of the young, romantic hero William Smith O'Brien and the newspaper mogul Sir John Gray. Oisín Kelly's statue of Jim Larkin, unveiled in 1979, was yet to come. But prime among the monuments in 1945 was the aforementioned Nelson's Pillar, which dominated the whole street.

During, and for four years after the end of World War II, the Pillar was the great terminus of the Dublin trams, 330 of which fanned out from here on thirty-one routes across the city and suburbs. They were the main vehicles for public transport, though rather slow moving, which was one of the complaints against them. They had earlier been replaced by buses, which were faster, but were re-introduced during World War II – or what was euphemistically called 'the Emergency' – when fuel practically ran out in 1941. It was mainly gardaí, politicians, doctors and priests who were given the few drops of petrol that could be got. The only native fuel available was turf won by Bord na Móna, a semi-state body founded in the 1930s to open up the bogs, and thousands of tons of it

THE METROPOLE AND THE EASON'S BUILDING

The area immediately to the south of the GPO was severely damaged during the Easter Rising. On the extreme right of this detail is the site of the Hotel Metropole, originally four Georgian houses that were combined in the early 1890s into a single building, fully rendered over the brick. Topped off with an elaborate balustrade and dormers, it had a French air. After 1916 it was rebuilt as the Metropole Restaurant and Cinema (seen here), designed by Aubrey O'Rourke. It was demolished in the 1970s to build a very plain department store and offices. In the centre is the Eason's building of 1919, designed by J. A. Ruthven; its landmark clock was not yet present in 1945.

TURNING THE CORNER

The corner of Sackville (O'Connell) Street and Eden Quay was completely destroyed in 1916. It had previously been well preserved, with eight original five-storey houses forming the corner and reaching as far as the massive, late Victorian Dublin Bread Company building on the Sackville (O'Connell) Street side. Here we see what was rebuilt after 1919, when the decision was made to create a boulevard befitting a capital city. On the eastern side of the city's major thoroughfare there was some flexibility in the roofline. In looking for a term to describe this style, the late Maurice Craig wittily coined 'neon-classical', a reference to cinema buildings that drew on classical architecture.

were transported by train to Dublin to keep the home fires burning, stored in large stacks in the Phoenix Park.

The trams were powered from overhead powerlines, fuelled by electricity from the Pigeon House station at the mouth of the Liffey. Coal was a rare commodity, rationed like so many other things during the Emergency. Partially responsible for this was De Valera's insistence on Irish neutrality, which did not dispose the British well towards providing Ireland with goods of various kinds. The importation of raw materials was heavily restricted as a result, so unemployment soared and many Irish men were forced to go to England in search of work.

One of the forgotten aspects of rationing was the distribution of ration books with coupons (often sold on the black market). These were particularly useful for buying clothes, but what hit broad swathes of the population most forcibly was the scanty supply of coupons with which to buy tea, the staple drink of most of Dublin's women, but also of the men who couldn't afford to buy porter.

For military reasons, the press, and even private post, was censored, which, together with restrictions on foreign travel — made more difficult by the war anyway — tended to create a somewhat claustrophobic atmosphere in the city. This was, however, partially made up for by an increase in theatrical entertainment and orchestral concerts, and the new Irish Exhibition of Living Art was formed as a protest against many of the conservative old stagers.

Rationing and the continuing use of overcrowded tenements – many within a stone's throw of O'Connell Street – had a devastating effect on the poorer elements of the city's population. Diseases such as typhus reappeared, and the subsequent campaign to eradicate the scourge of tuberculosis had not yet begun in 1945, causing many to suffer and subsequently die from it. Infant mortality, too, rose again, to the considerable unease of the city's health authorities.

But the populace still went about their daily chores and got to their jobs by tram – or by bicycles, which suddenly became very common and had a city-centre revival. Looking at old pictures of Dublin around this time, one is struck by the uniformity of men's clothing, invariably drab and dull. Women did their best with their coupons to buy clothes that brightened things up a bit – anything to get away from a life which had been restricted by rationing. Still, it took a long time to get over the effects of the 'economic war' with England.

THE PARNELL MONUMENT

This statue answers the O'Connell Monument at the other end of the street. The Parnell Monument is around six metres taller than O'Connell's, but Parnell has no attendant figures so the footprint is much smaller by comparison. The foundation stone was laid in 1899, before a sculptor had been commissioned; it took until 1911 for the monument to be completed, some twenty years after the death of Parnell.

It was designed by the American sculptor Augustus Saint-Gaudens, who had been born in Ireland, and it was paid for mostly by donations from the other side of the Atlantic. Originally planned as a four-sided structure, it was then changed to triangular. The table beside which the politician stands must have been thought necessary to avoid his figure being 'lost' against the massive granite shaft.

The monument to the 'uncrowned king of Ireland' was still under wraps during the final royal visit under British rule, made by King George V in July 1911. It was unveiled in October, and the following April, the third and final Home Rule Bill began its successful progress (although enactment of such legislation would be put on hold for the duration of World War I). The granite shaft bears a golden harp without a crown, now the coat of arms of modern Ireland.

This picture reveals the core of a city that had changed comparatively little between the mid-nineteenth and mid-twentieth centuries, and that was still in the grip of an economic depression. World War II had fortunately come to an end five years previously, but its effects were still to be felt. Food rationing was at an end, and I remember as a child my amazement upon being offered an orange for the first time – the same year that I heard of the assassination of Mahatma Gandhi, which meant nothing to me back then. The continued stagnation of the economy resulted in forced emigration from the city and the country generally. One of the few firms succeeding in the export trade was Arthur Guinness, the top of one of whose buildings you can just about see to the left of the dome of the Four Courts in the upper right-hand corner of the picture. But what is the giveaway in their activity here is the barge chugging slowly upstream, with its throaty, thumping sound. It is near O'Connell Bridge at low tide and has dipped its funnel to proceed underneath and continue on up to the brewery to get further supplies. O'Connell Street, at the centre right of the main picture, had recovered from the severe shelling from the gunboat *Helga* that had come up the Liffey in 1916, and had brightened things up by painting some of the buildings white.

After the retirement of the trams in 1949, the buses, double- and single-deckered, were back in the streets, in a rather sombre dark green with a stripe to alleviate the boredom. Cars in the city numbered around 25,000, and the cessation of petrol rationing was to lead to a gradual increase in the following decade. Real traffic chaos

1. PROVOST'S HOUSE, TRINITY COLLEGE, DUBLIN (TCD)

2. GRAFTON STREET

3. APSE OF THE COLLEGE CHAPEL, TCD

4. PEDIMENT OF FRONT GATE, TCD

5. THEATRE ROYAL, DEMOLISHED 1962

6. CORN EXCHANGE, DESIGNED BY GEORGE HALPIN IN 1815. FAÇADE RECENTLY DISFIGURED BY THE ADDITION OF A CENTRAL DOOR

7. MERCER'S HOSPITAL

8. ST. ANDREW'S CHURCH

9. COLLEGE GREEN

10. COPPER-COVERED ROOF OF THE BANK OF IRELAND, FORMERLY PARLIAMENT HOUSE

11. ST. PATRICK'S CATHEDRAL

12. SITE OF ELEVEN-STOREY O'CONNELL BRIDGE HOUSE (1965)

13. BALLAST OFFICE, REBUILT AS A REPLICA IN THE EARLY 1980S

14. DUBLIN CASTLE

15. ST. NICHOLAS OF MYRA CHURCH

16. CITY HALL, BUILT AS THE ROYAL EXCHANGE

17. NEWCOMEN BANK, BUILT 1781, NOW THE RATES OFFICE OF DUBLIN CITY COUNCIL

18. O'CONNELL BRIDGE

19. GUINNESS BARGE WITH HINGED SMOKESTACK

20. CHRIST CHURCH CATHEDRAL

21. TOWER OF ST. MICHAEL'S CHURCH

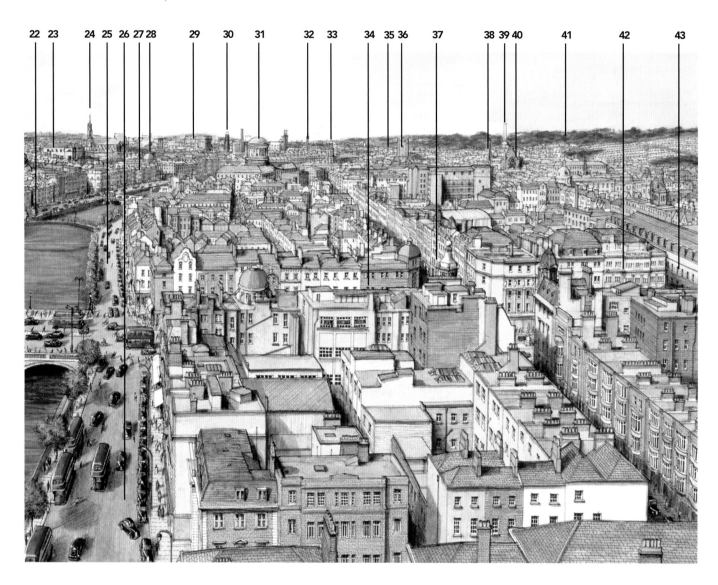

22. THE HA'PENNY BRIDGE

23. ST. AUDOEN'S CATHOLIC CHURCH

24. CHURCH OF ST. AUGUSTINE AND ST. JOHN, THOMAS STREET

25. BACHELORS WALK

26. EDEN QUAY

27. WOOD QUAY

28. ADAM & EVE'S, THE FRANCISCAN CHURCH

29. GUINNESS BREWERY

30. FORMER WINDMILL BELONGING TO ROE'S DISTILLERY

31. THE FOUR COURTS

32. ROYAL HOSPITAL, KILMAINHAM

33. ST. PAUL'S, ARRAN QUAY

34. LOWER O'CONNELL STREET

35. HEUSTON (FORMERLY KINGSBRIDGE) RAILWAY STATION

36. ST. MICHAN'S CHURCH

37. MIDDLE ABBEY STREET

38. CHIMNEY OF JAMESON'S DISTILLERY

39. WELLINGTON MONUMENT

40. ST. MARY OF THE ANGELS CHURCH

41 PHOENIX PARK

42. METROPOLE RESTAURANT AND CINEMA

43. SOUTH SIDE OF THE GPO

was far into the future, however, and at this time cars were driven up and down the Quays in both directions.

But the best way to study how the city has flourished in the last fifty years is by noticing what is *not* in this picture. Perhaps chronologically one of the first events not visible was the placing of the 'bowl of light' on a raised platform in the middle of O'Connell Bridge in April 1953. (It was thrown into the Liffey, as a student prank, only a few weeks later.) Its purpose was to celebrate a new festival, An Tóstal, a tourism initiative designed to lure those Irish who had emigrated within the last two decades back home, at least temporarily. It succeeded in doing so for a while, and though it fizzled out in Dublin by 1958, it was, nevertheless, a first step in reinvigorating a tourist industry which was to forge ahead in leaps and bounds in the ensuing decades. As An Tóstal was coming to an end, the Dublin Theatre Festival was drawing the ire and fire of the Catholic archbishop John Charles McQuaid, who succeeded in stopping the 1958 festival because he saw its contents as inimical to his views on keeping pure the morals of the population. Until his death in 1972, McQuaid wielded unbelievable power, and, being anti-Protestant and a repressor of sexuality, he could well have been described as a killjoy who wanted his hierarchy to dominate every aspect of Irish family life, both inside and outside politics.

But the year of the abandoned festival also saw the publication of a Programme for Economic Expansion which, unusually for a civil-service paper, appeared under the name of its author, T.K. Whitaker, head of the Department of Finance (and decades later named Greatest Living Irish Person!). With the political will of the Taoiseach of the time, Seán Lemass, to push its ideas forward, it heralded the end of De Valera's protectionist era and the start of a new investment strategy that was to turn the tide around and raise all boats with it.

The streetscape that this picture illustrates shows houses rarely more than four storeys high, which keep a fairly uniform skyline. But, in the 1960s, the pattern began to be broken with the abrupt introduction of the seventeen-storey Liberty Hall of 1965, which rises to a height of sixty metres. Had the artist wanted to show the city in 1965 rather than 1950, this is what the view would have been like from the top of Liberty Hall, but with a few important additions. The buildings in the bottom right of the picture would have been in the process of demolition to make way for Michael Scott and Ronald Tallon's Abbey (and smaller Peacock) Theatre of 1966. The Abbey had originally been on the same site but was burned down in 1951, forcing the acting troupe and management to move temporarily to the Queen's Theatre in Pearse Street. On the opposite bank of the river, the old Theatre Royal was replaced by the ugly monstrosity of Hawkins House in 1963, and only a few years later Desmond Fitzgerald's eleven-storey O'Connell Bridge House raised a not-very-attractive head above the adjoining rooftops on the corner of Burgh Quay and D'Olier Street. Perhaps even more noticeable was the addition on Dame Street of the Central Bank (1971–1978) by Sam Stephenson, an ingenious construction whereby the seven floors were hauled up by steel hangers. Unfortunately, the building went higher than was allowed in the planning permission, which subsequently forced the Bank to eliminate one of the floors.

Another feature which has changed Dublin life since 1950 is the addition of a number of new bridges, of which only two need to be mentioned here. The first is Rosie Hackett Bridge, below O'Connell Bridge, which joins Hawkins Street to the bottom of Marlborough Street, and which is planned to carry the Luas line across the Liffey.

The other is the pedestrian Millennium Bridge – upstream from the equally pedestrian Ha'penny Bridge – by Howley Harrington Architects and Price & Myers engineers. In addition, we now have attractive wooden walkways extending outwards over the river on the north side, parallel with the Quays, which add a lovely and swingy touch and help us to get away from the car fumes just over the wall.

Finally, it may be noted that, since 1950, the city has extended far beyond its boundaries of that time, creating large satellite suburban townships at places like Clondalkin and Tallaght on the south side and Ballymun on the north, some of which took up residents from the dreadfully overcrowded city-centre tenements in the 1950s and 1960s. We can only be thankful that we are not living in the Dublin of the 1950s!

THE ARMS OF THE
CORPORATION OF DUBLIN

The Corporation of Dublin grew out of medieval local government from the thirteenth century and consisted of a lord mayor, aldermen and burgesses. In 2002,
it officially became Dublin City Council, a name that had first been used for the
single-chamber governing body from 1840. Although many job descriptions —
including alderman and town clerk — had disappeared by 2002, the honorific
title of lord mayor has been retained.

This version of the coat of arms had to be reduced to fit the pediment of the
Mansion House, the official residence of the lord mayor since 1715, so the
supporters (figures that stand on either side of the arms) are missing — but
they have left their attributes behind. The shield in the centre shows on a blue
background three castles — or, more probably, city gates — on fire; watchtowers
and a gate also appear on the Dublin City Seal of around 1230. The attributes
surrounding the shield include the scales of justice, the Great Dublin Civic Sword from
the fourteenth century, and the Great Mace of Dublin dating from the early eighteenth century, which includes parts of an earlier mace. The
brown fur hat on the top is particular to lord mayors in heraldry. The motto says, in effect, that obedience by its citizens makes for a happy city.

EXPAN
EDUC

UCD

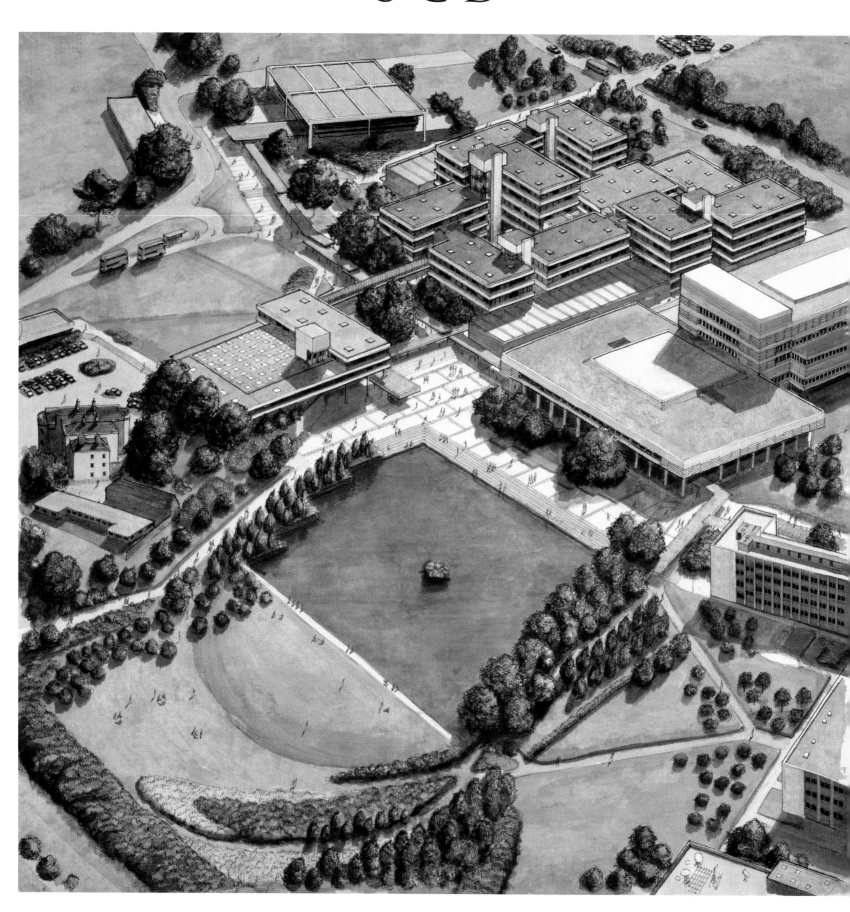

Comparable to its centre-city counterpart in Trinity College, University College, Dublin, spans three centuries of fine architecture but, in this case, leading up to the largest conglomeration of modern buildings on a single green-field site anywhere in the country, as seen in the accompanying illustration. The story starts with numbers 85 and 86 St. Stephen's Green, built in 1738 and 1765 respectively, which were taken over in the opposite order for use as the Catholic University of Ireland, founded in 1854, with John Henry, Cardinal Newman, as its first rector. Because it was not in a position to award degrees, it was linked in 1879 to a new examining body, the Royal University, but the Catholic University did not flourish and (minus its medical school) was taken over by the Jesuits. That same year, 1883, the establishment in St. Stephen's Green became University College, a title it still retains today. But it moved premises in 1914 to Earlsfort Terrace, just around the corner, where its Great Hall (from an earlier building) now serves as the National Concert Hall.

Particularly when the new State had begun to settle down after the Civil War, the number of students in University College began to rise dramatically, and it was clear by my time there in the 1950s that the existing buildings were inadequate. Michael Tierney, the president at the time, cast around to see whither he could move his college to provide adequate space and room for students. During the time of his predecessor Denis Coffey, the college had acquired a sizeable estate at Belfield on the Stillorgan Road, some four miles south-east of Earlsfort Terrace, as a sports centre with playing

WEJCHERT'S MASTERPLAN

The core of Andrzej Wejchert's masterplan is seen
here in the mid-1980s, since when the number
of buildings on site and their capacity has more
than doubled. Rather than placing a series of
unconnected buildings in parkland, Wejchert sought
to create a 'high street' that would give the new
campus a greater sense of identity. He also included
around six hundred metres of covered walkways. In
the top left is the restaurant building by Robin Walker
(1968–1970), a very successful structure with a flexible
interior. Centre right is the masterplan's centrepiece,
the arts and commerce building, now called the
Newman Building. The library, bottom right, is now
named after James Joyce.

fields. This was to be the first of a total of eleven houses and gardens which the college subsequently bought as they came up for sale. They were amalgamated into an area of some three hundred acres, which preserved seven of the older houses that still decorate the grounds. It was here, then, that Tierney and others chose to re-locate the college. As a result, the centre of the city lost a university, and UCD cut itself off from the core of Dublin urban life – but with the advantage of gaining plenty more space for staff and students.

The change of location was ratified by Dáil Éireann, the Irish parliament, in 1960, and because space for science students was at a premium in Dublin city, it was decided to forge ahead – without any architectural competition – and construct a set of new science buildings on the green-field site, designed by the Irish architect Joseph V. Downes. The two buildings on the bottom right of the main picture formed part of that new science complex, consisting of separate structures for chemistry, biology and physics, with lecture halls in the centre. The first sod was turned in June 1962 in the presence of President Éamon de Valera, Taoiseach Seán Lemass, Archbishop John Charles McQuaid and, of course, UCD President Michael Tierney, whose brainchild it was and who retired the day the science building was opened in 1964. He must have felt that moving the university to Belfield was his finest achievement.

To start with one building before a plan could be worked out for the whole campus was rather jumping the gun and, as a result, an architectural competition was announced to find a suitable design for the layout of whole site, but which would obviously have to take account of the presence of the new building. Six assessors, three of international renown, were chosen to oversee the competition, for which 105 entries were received by the closing date, which was just before the opening of the science building in 1964. There must have been some raised eyebrows when it emerged that the winner was a young Polish architect, Andrzej Wejchert, a graduate of the Faculty of Architecture of Warsaw Polytechnic. For his entry, he was highly praised for arranging his buildings on either side of a pedestrian mall, which rises and falls with the ground level, and which provides access off it to different sections of the campus. Part of the prize for winning the competition was the opportunity to design one of the planned buildings, and so Wejchert got the contract to construct one of the largest of the college's complexes, the arts and commerce building, a horizontally stratified group of

three-storey square and rectangular structures, seen at the centre-right of the detail opposite. It was opened in 1970, again by De Valera, amid protests from students and Maoists. To the left and slightly below, as we look at it, is another Wejchert-designed building, the two-level administrative centre with an almost central tower rising from the lower-level roof, which was opened in 1972. In the same year Wejchert pulled off a remarkable and difficult achievement: the sixty-metre-high UCD water tower, containing 150,000 gallons of water and compared to 'a massive torch of learning' visible for miles around. With his UCD success, Wejchert opened an office in Dublin and stayed in Ireland for the rest of his life, designing many other iconic buildings including his last, the museum in Glasnevin Cemetery, where he showed his masterful use of light.

The administration centre fronts on to the artificial

PERIOD HOUSES ON THE CAMPUS OF UCD
The several estates that were united to form the new campus of UCD were known for the beauty of their settings and formal gardens. In the late 1990s, UCD implemented a 'Programme for the Preservation of Period Houses'. Seen here is the rear of one of them, Ardmore, designed by John McCurdy. Others include Merville House, built circa 1750 for Anthony Foster, Chief Baron of the Irish Exchequer, and the neo-Gothic Roebuck Castle, dating from 1854. In 1934, one of the first acquisitions was Belfield House, which sits on an elevated site with views out to Dublin Bay. It dates from 1801, with later extensions, and is home to an institute within the university.

lake in the lower centre of the main picture, which is where Wejchert's mall takes off into the background at the top left. There, at the far end, is the flat, square restaurant with eight-part roof, designed by Robin Walker of Scott Tallon Walker and inspired by Ludwig Mies van der Rohe, who influenced Walker's practice very much, as witnessed by his Bank of Ireland Headquarters on Baggot Street. But the largest building looking directly on to the lake is the library, flat in front but higher behind, the product of the Scottish practice of J. Hardie Glover, which was founded by the famous architect Sir Basil Spence and specialised in university libraries. Before it was completed, students – in the aftermath of uprisings in Paris and elsewhere in 1968 – protested bitterly to the college authorities that, while teaching had already been transferred to Belfield, the contents of the library had not, and they were dissatisfied that only temporary library arrangements were available for the undergraduates. The library was finished in due course and a phase two envisaged, but government finance became a difficulty for construction in the 1980s. The picture here represents the stage of building as it was in 1985, and a number of buildings completed after that date are not included. But what does feature in the centre left of the picture is Ardmore, one of the seven houses to survive from the time before Belfield became a university campus, having been built in 1871 by John McCurdy, who also designed the east wing of Kilmainham Gaol.

The Belfield campus is remarkable, among other things, for having assembled an international selection of architects to house the administration and the various faculties. This very fact shows that Ireland of the 1960s was beginning to climb out of its isolationist lethargy, and to take its place in an international field. Office-block design had first got a modern boost with Michael Scott's Busáras in the 1950s, with an international style being introduced by John Johansen in the American Embassy and Paul Koralek in the new Berkeley Library and Arts Building in Trinity. But UCD can claim to have got the first big cohort of national and international architects to provide a great variety of styles on a single green-field site in a very attractive, modern idiom. Their work was unrivalled in the rest of the country until the emergence of the University of Limerick in the following decade, and fits in remarkably well with Wejchert's original ideal.

JAMES JOYCE
AS A STUDENT

Joyce stands outside 85 St. Stephen's Green. He graduated with a B.A. in 1902, too early to have studied in Earlsfort Terrace, University College's larger premises around the corner. His later schooling had been in Belvedere College, a private Jesuit second-ary school for boys on Great Denmark Street, not far from the top of Sackville (O'Connell) Street. The school occupied Belvedere House, built in 1774 by George Augustus Rochfort, later second Earl of Belvedere, with interior stucco decoration by Michael Stapleton. Moving to 85 and 86 St. Stephen's Green, Joyce must have felt quite at home, as these fine buildings were of a slightly earlier vintage than Belvedere and also boasted stucco decoration, by the Lafranchini brothers and Robert West.

There are photographs of Joyce on the day of his graduation, sitting for a group photograph in the gardens behind numbers 85 and 86.

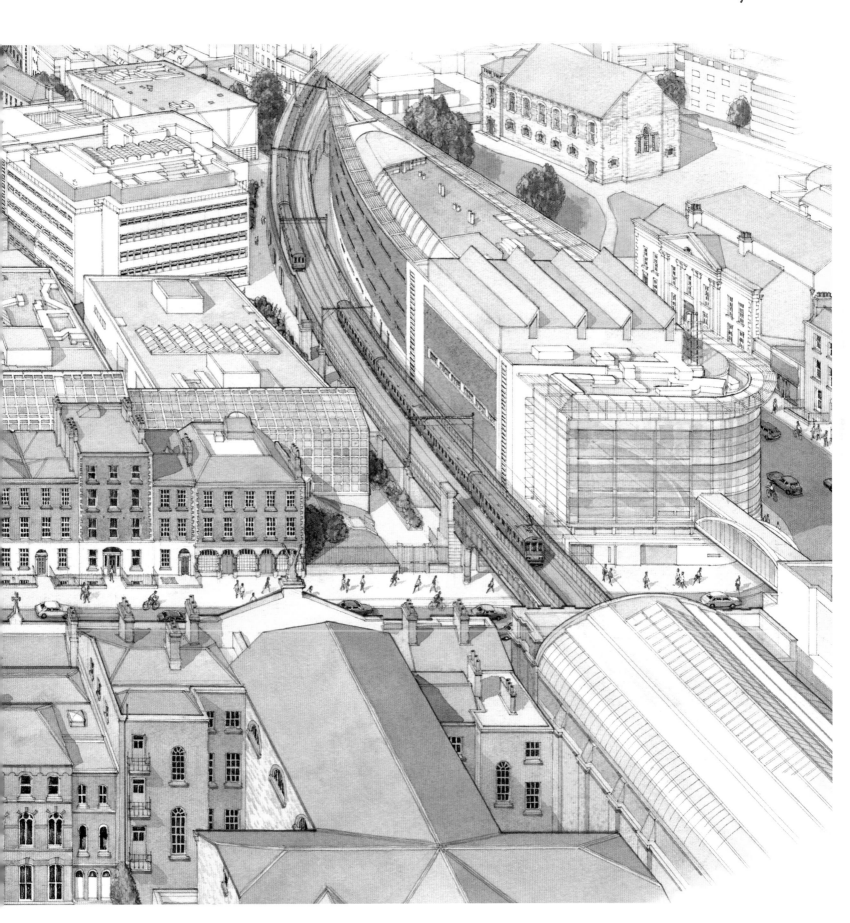

hen the Duke of Leinster built Leinster House (now the Dáil and the Seanad) in 1745 and suggested that where he went, others would follow, he was right! To go down the street from it and follow the walls of Trinity College to the east, one comes to Westland Row, originally called Westland's Row after a long-forgotten property owner, William Westland, when it opened in 1773. Two years earlier, however, a County Wicklow builder named Nicholas Tench took a site and built upon it the only significant eighteenth-century house on the street, which was leased in 1780 to Sir Samuel Bradstreet, the City Recorder. Perhaps his title was prophetic because, if you pass the house today, you are likely to hear recorders and other instruments being played within by youthful musicians; the premises has been the venerable Royal Irish Academy of Music for almost a century and a half, and the nursery of many of Ireland's important instrumentalists and soloists ever since. It is also claimed that it was the townhouse of the Marquess Conyngham, whose wife was the mistress of King George IV.

But Westland Row has other important claims to fame. On its eastern side, adjoining the metal bridge — its roof is seen in the bottom right of the main picture — is the railway station named in honour of the Pearse family, including executed Easter Rising leaders Willie and Pádraig, after whom the street mentioned below is also named. It was from this station in 1834 that Ireland's first railway line led from the capital city to Kingstown, which later reverted to the name Dún Laoghaire. Kingstown was the docking port for boats bringing the mail from England and Wales, and the train was

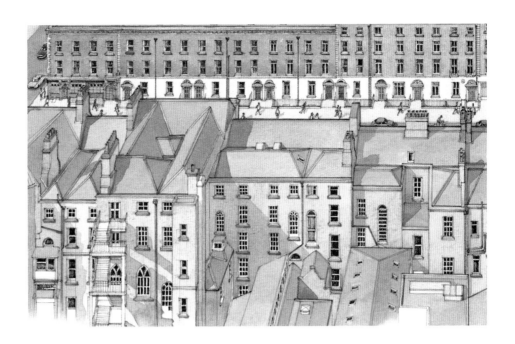

WHAT LIES BEHIND

Looking at the rear of Dublin's Georgian buildings can be enlightening. In the bottom left of this detail, we see the back of the Royal Irish Academy of Music, with two Gothic-style windows on the first floor. It could be that the lady of the house preferred the 'Strawberry Hill Gothic' look for her morning room, while the front elevation has rounded windows in the classical vein. Georgian houses lacked built-in plumbing, so in some cases bathrooms have been added in the form of a cantilevered room or other extension leading from the staircase landing. On the other side of the street, top right, can be seen the house where Oscar Wilde was born. This whole range of buildings has been preserved by Trinity College and integrated into the large new structures behind.

seen as a speedy way of getting the post to Dublin, whose port had so silted up that larger boats found it difficult to dock there at the time. This new, faster form of transport – spouting smoke, unlike the horse-drawn omnibus cabs in use in the city at the time – must have seemed like the magical embodiment of the new industrial era in the eyes of the startled citizens. They enjoyed the railway so much that they started building new suburbs at the recently created stations where the train stopped en route. Within decades, other new railway termini evolved to serve lines leading from the capital to the north, south and west of the country. Various plans were suggested to join all the stations together, with one branching off at Sydney Parade and running under the Liffey. It never happened, however, and in 1891 Westland Row became no longer just a terminus but a station on a line extending over a bridge across the river to Amiens Street via Tara Street. It was to facilitate this enterprise that the decorative metal bridge was built across Westland Row, and it still serves its purpose to this day, a century and a quarter later.

Contemporary with the station building is St. Andrew's Church, on which work began in 1832, a fine Doric

structure designed by John Bolger, with a T-shaped interior above a series of underfloor vaults. Its classical design followed the Greek façade of the Pro-Cathedral in Marlborough Street, and it was the first Dublin Catholic church to have been built on a main thoroughfare. The original plan, it appears, had the entrance onto narrow Cumberland Street behind it, in order to get the government to allow the building to proceed, since Catholic churches normally had to face onto smaller streets. However, as soon as permission was granted, the entrance was changed so as to face onto Westland Row, where the gable top was decorated with a statue of St. Andrew by John Smyth, son of the famous Edward who had decorated James Gandon's classical buildings in the city. The man who was largely responsible for acquiring the site for the church, and for the fundraising necessary to build it, was none other than the Liberator, Daniel O'Connell, who donated the baptismal font — which had originally been designed as a wine cooler!

St. Andrew's was the focal point of a parish which stretched southwards to include Merrion Square, the location of O'Connell's Dublin home. Of the famous doctors who lived on the square, including William Stokes and Robert Graves, only Dominic Corrigan was a Catholic who would have worshipped in St. Andrew's. More famous was Sir William Wilde, whose remarkable achievements are listed on a beautiful plaque between the windows of the ground floor of his residence at number I Merrion Square. He moved there in the late 1850s from number 21 Westland Row, almost opposite St. Andrew's, which is where his more famous son, Oscar, was born in 1854. Towards the end of the century, Oscar took the literary and, more particularly, the theatrical world in London by storm with his enchanting comedies before being hounded out of society for having had a homosexual relationship.

Oscar's birth is recorded on a marble plaque on number 21, which is part of a long terrace of early Victorian houses on the western side of Westland Row that have been acquired, and thereby preserved, by Trinity College. That same university has also purchased many of the buildings in the street at right angles to Westland Row, namely Pearse Street, formerly Great Brunswick Street, which can be seen in the upper right-hand corner of the main picture. In the nineteenth century, this was a hive

of cultural activity of various kinds. It contributed to the city's musical life through the classical-fronted building seen in the centre-right of the detail below, which began its existence as the offices of the Dublin Oil Gas Company but was transformed into the Antient Concert Rooms in the 1840s. As its title implied, it concentrated on the choral classics by Handel, Haydn, Mozart and Mendelssohn, but also played host to instrumentalists including Clara Schumann, Joseph Joachim and Anton Rubinstein. Singers of calibre who appeared there included Swedish opera singer Jenny Lind, the renowned Limerick soprano Catherine Hayes, and the great Athlone-born tenor John

COLLEGE NEIGHBOURS

The roof of St. Andrew's Church and the span of the station's roof can be seen at the bottom here. In the middle right is the frontage of what was the Antient Concert Rooms, and at the top, in the centre, is St. Mark's Church. Modern Pearse Street between D'Olier Street and Westland Row is much later than its eastward extent towards the Grand Canal Basin; at the end of the eighteenth century, there were still gardens and fields here, including the Vice Provost's garden. St. Mark's ceased to be an Anglican church in 1971 and was bought by Trinity College. In 1987, it was sold again and is now a Pentecostal church. Oscar Wilde was baptised here.

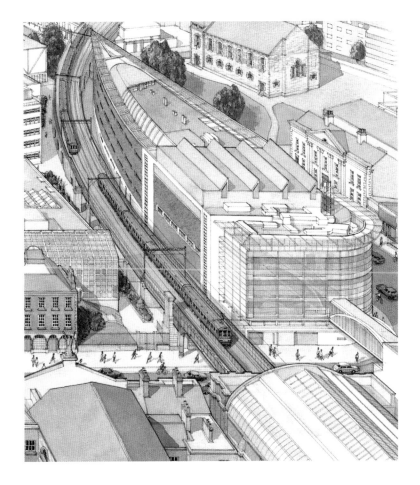

McCormack, who shared a platform there with James Joyce in 1904 (the year in which he set *Ulysses*). In 1899, the building staged the first performance of the Irish Literary Theatre which, five years later, developed into the Abbey Theatre. The Abbey would later have a further connection with Pearse Street because, when it burned down in 1951, its productions were moved to the Queen's Theatre at number 209, before moving back to its re-built home on Abbey Street, north of the Liffey, in 1966.

Pearse Street gets its name from the patriot Pádraig Pearse, executed in 1916, whose father had a monument works where the railway loop-line crosses the street, and whose brother William contributed to the sculpture of St. Andrew's Church. Another parishioner of the church was John Hogan, who produced a beautiful memorial to Jeanette Farrell within the church.

Almost the entire upper part of the main picture is taken up with the eastern end of Trinity College, which has changed beyond all recognition within the last quarter of a century. (For a very different view of the campus, captured around the year 1780, see p. 88.) The expe-

rienced eye will pick out some of the older stone-built, gable-roofed buildings housing the botany, physiology, zoology and other departments, but these now have been almost engulfed in the great variety of modern structures. Among the earliest of these is Luce Hall of 1979, to the left of the loop-line, recently demolished to make way for a new business school. Embraced by the curve of the railway line is the Naughton Institute and Sports Centre, shaped like the prow of a ship and also encompassing the very successful Science Gallery, initiated by Michael John Gorman. The flat-roofed cement buildings forming the centre of the picture include the O'Reilly (1989) and Lloyd (2003) Institutes as well as the Hamilton Building (1994). The red-brick building near the upper left-hand corner is School of Dental Science, while the L-shaped building nearby is the Moyne Institute, which looks out over College Park. This green swathe, seen in the top left of our illustration, provides breathing space for cricket and rugby, contrasting with the remarkable close-knit building activity that has been taking place between it and Westland Row since the 1980s.

OSCAR WILDE OUTSIDE
1 MERRION SQUARE

When he was still an infant, the family of Oscar Wilde moved from Westland Row to number 1 Merrion Square; this house not only has a plaque to Wilde but also a multi-coloured jade and marble statue in the gardens opposite. Danny Osborne, an Irish sculptor, was commissioned by the Guinness Ireland group, and the statue was placed there in 1997.

In some ways the life of Oscar's father, Sir William Robert Wills Wilde, paralleled that of his son. At first, all went very well with his education and career, and marriage and children followed. But then a disastrous court case relating to an alleged sexual incident involving Sir William was a great scandal and nearly bankrupted the household. He had three illegitimate children whom he acknowledged but who were reared by relatives.

We see Oscar here as a young man at Trinity College, before he left for Magdalen College Oxford, at which stage his clothing took a decidedly eccentric turn. On his tour to America, he became famous for his long hair and breeches, part of his 'aesthetic garb'.

SMITHFIELD

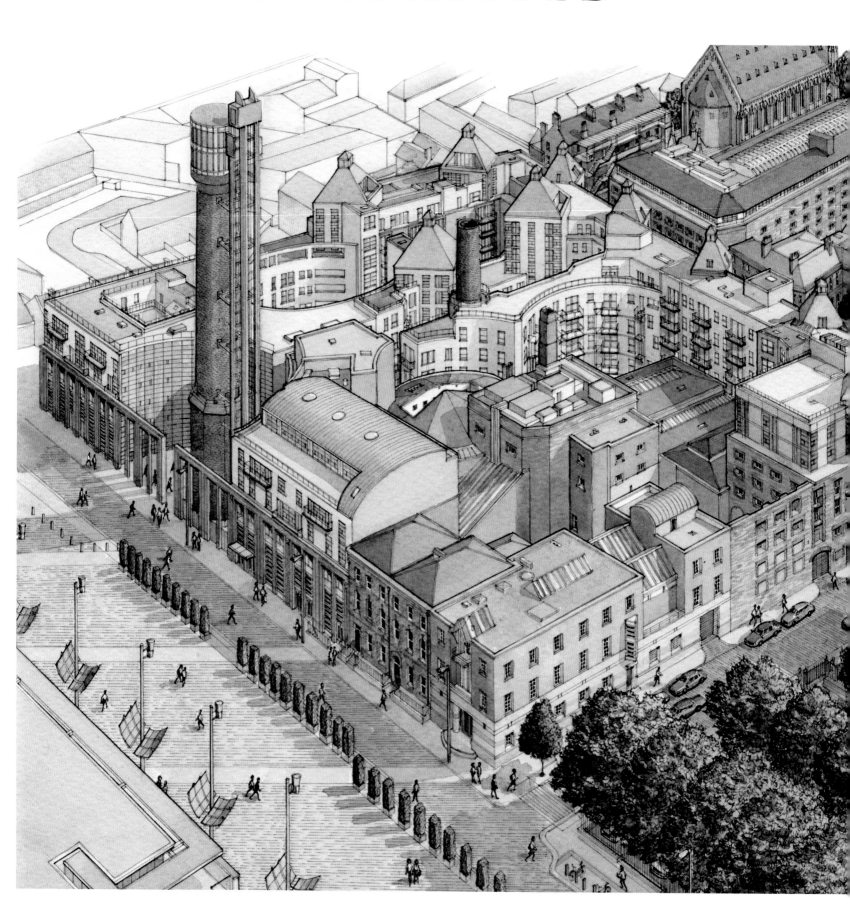

S mithfield, a part of which makes up the triangle at the bottom left of the main picture, probably derived its name from its counterpart in London when first developed in the 1660s. The whole area belonged to the Dublin district known as Oxmantown, a part of the city which was originally settled by the Norse ('East-men') as they moved northwards across the Liffey in the eleventh century, before others of their kinsmen were ejected from the city with the arrival of the Normans in 1170. Some of their traces were discovered in an excavation carried out in the triangular space in the extreme right-hand portion of the main picture. At its northern end, a Hiberno-Norse house from the eleventh century came to light – the earliest evidence so far of Viking habitation north of the river – on the site of a much older Bronze Age cooking place. The house may well have been one of a whole row of houses extending along what is now Church Street, seen running diagonally at the top of the picture. Further towards the north, this led to the church of St. Michan, whose square, medieval-looking Gothic tower with cross-topped roof can be seen in the detail opposite. For five hundred years, it was the only Protestant urban parish church north of the Liffey, called after one of those obscure saints whose origins are much discussed but never resolved. Was he an Irish saint or a Norseman venerated by his countrymen, who are said to have founded the church in 1095 – the century that would have seen what is regarded as the strongest Christianisation of the pagan Vikings? For Dubliners, the church is most famous for the leathery remains of ancient citizens in its subterranean vaults, normally referred to as medieval Cru-

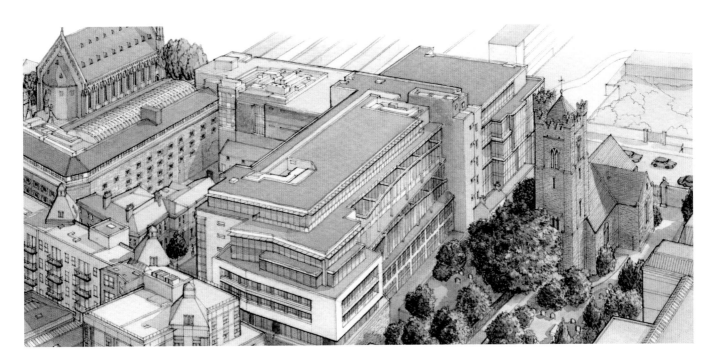

SERVICE INDUSTRIES: CHURCHES AND OFFICES

St. Mary of the Angels Church and St. Michan's are seen here, separated by a large office building, the Kings Building on Church Street. This was built by a father-and-son team, both named John Byrne, and lay empty for years after its completion in 2008. Mr Byrne Senior developed other city-centre sites including O'Connell Bridge House (1965) on the corner of D'Olier Street and Burgh Quay, which thrusts high above the older buildings of the country's most important urban space. At least this more recent Byrne structure stays within range of the roofline of other buildings nearby. In 2015 much of the office space was let to an American software company, a sign of revival in the economy.

saders, a reputation they may have got for being seemingly rather tall. Their remarkable preservation is due to the tannic acid content of what was once a rather marshy, undrained area. But they could (disappointingly) be from no earlier than the seventeenth century, to which the oldest part of the present church may be assigned. That it is probably the successor to one or more earlier churches is suggested by the presence of the effigy of a twelfth- or thirteenth-century bishop inside the church.

The organ is said by some to have been played by Handel when he came to Dublin for the first performance of his

Messiah in 1742. But even if this is not true, music buffs will find recompense in the fine trophy of a variety of instruments carved in 1724 for the organ loft.

St. Michan's has been Protestant since the sixteenth century; its attractive, and much later, Catholic counterpart, St. Mary of the Angels, is the Gothic-apsed structure seen to the left of the detail above. This is a friary of the Capuchin order, designed by the famous Victorian architect J.J. McCarthy in 1881. Between them, the two churches reflected the popularity of their respective religions. St. Michan's, and also St. Paul's (on North King Street, as

RELICS OF INDUSTRY

The Smithfield area demonstrates how older industrial buildings can be reused. In the Dublin of the 1960s and 1970s, it is likely that all the old distillery buildings surviving here would have been swept away as serving no purpose. Instead the three chimneys were retained and serve as landmarks for the new complex that incorporates several older buildings, while also allowing the architects to create modern shops, offices and apartments.

distinct from the Catholic church on Arran Quay depicted on p. 164), were centres of worship for the Protestant population of the original parish of St. Michan's. They made up the majority of the inhabitants throughout the eighteenth century, during the first half of which this area was one of the most vibrant and rapidly expanding suburbs of Dublin. Development had started around 1664, when the Duke of Ormonde was making his mark on the city (see the Royal Hospital, Kilmainham, p. 124). The area around Smithfield was divided up into ninety-six plots, and these were let out to prominent citizens, who must have been disappointed when the Duke did not take up the allotment of seven acres which had been granted to him. It was the intention of Dublin Corporation that Smithfield should become one of the city's important residential areas, but

it was competing against St. Stephen's Green on the south side, which was becoming more popular after the Duke of Leinster built his mansion in neighbouring Kildare Street in 1745. More significantly, the same period saw the rise of Henrietta Street (p. 134) not far away on the north side, which attracted the nobility as Smithfield had signally failed to do, possibly because of the odours of cattle and horses brought to Smithfield Market from beyond the city's boundary. The animals were herded thither by Catholic drovers coming from Meath and Kildare, who settled there, gradually integrating with the local population and creating a Catholic majority during the course of the nineteenth century that has remained to this day. The horse-fair tradition of the eighteenth century continued until recent times, but is now reduced to just a trickle.

The Lord Mayor's bye-laws promulgated for Smithfield in 1854 give some idea of the atmosphere of the place at the time. The southern end, near the bottom of the main picture, was a haymarket, where hay and straw were bundled into trusses, and each cart carrying them into the market was weighed by a weigh-master. Not just horses but cattle, sheep and pigs were to be sold. Between noon on one day and 9 a.m. on the next, it was permitted to have pens erected to protect one's property. Anyone who brought in animals 'so unsound or disordered as to be unfit for human food' was to be fined £5.

The proximity of the soldiers living in Collins Barracks certainly helped to promote the trade in horses, but it also encouraged prostitution – and the spread of taverns supplying whiskey galore. So it is appropriate that the building block seen in the detail on the opposite page should be occupied by the former Jameson distillery, now a popular tourist attraction. Here visitors flock to get a taste of the product and see the workings of the old distillery, going back largely to the nineteenth century. It was recorded in 1887 that the distillery employed three hundred men and produced one million gallons of whiskey per annum. Its most eye-catching structure is the boiler-house chimney of 1895, which was converted in the 1990s for use as a splendid viewing tower, providing a panoramic vista over the city's expanse, but this function has been sadly suspended in recent years. The visitor centre has some interesting features such as the large copper vat and wash backs, where fermentation formerly took place, though the distillery itself was moved a number of years ago to Midleton in County Cork.

By the 1990s, Smithfield had become quite run down,

LIFE ON THE SQUARE

Smithfield is equipped with a small stage, and the masts are sometimes lit from below to provide a colourful display. There are occasional events here, organised by Dublin City Council, but there is something lacking; residents living in the apartments have no escape when sound reverberates around the enclosed space, or when an event brings in thousands of fans, or goes on too long. The Horse Fair may be confined to history, for the most part – it now takes place just twice a year – but residents will probably always want it as quiet in Smithfield as it currently seems to be. The Light House Cinema, with its four screens, certainly brings some life into the area.

with just a few garages and old shops that would have had little attraction for anyone to go there. But in the final years of the last millennium, Dublin Corporation decided to make it the centrepiece of what is described as an Historic Area Rejuvenation Plan or HARP (an abbreviation more closely associated with the product of a famous brewery on the other side of the Liffey). This plan changed particularly the western side of Smithfield, where the raggle-taggle of houses and commercial premises were redeveloped under a tax-incentive scheme as and from 1998, and this turned one side of the whole length of the open space into new premises, including shops and a hotel. The east side is now somewhat incongruously described as Smithfield Village, and it includes an interesting building of mixed use designed by A&D Wejchert (compare UCD, p. 198), which backs on to the distillery. What most strikes the visitor on entering Smithfield today are the 26.5-metre-high brazier masts, with large panels like sails halfway up, which, as Christine Casey remarked, 'would not have been out of place at a triumphalist military rally'! They may not be universally popular, but they do help to give a new face to what had become a rather neglected part of the city.

The whole area adjoining Smithfield has also been given a modern facelift. To the south, next to the trees near the bottom of the main picture, is a refurbished older structure called the Distillers Building, which contains commercial offices. Next to the Capuchin friary mentioned above, the Bar Council of Ireland has rejuvenated Church Street with their new Law Library. Smithfield's great advantage nowadays is that it is more easily accessible through the Red Line Luas, the electric tram car seen in the right-hand corner, which proclaims its name in English and Irish (*Margadh na Feirme*, literally 'the Farmers' Market') as one of the stops between O'Connell Street and Heuston Station.

A COPPER WHISKEY STILL

The Old Jameson Distillery has some handsome exhibits from the time when it was an important

employer in the area. This copper still would have contained the 'wash' that was heated up for making

whiskey, and is seen in isolation here. Following the principle of an ancient alembic, the still would

have had a copper arm connecting the top to a condensing unit. The largest-ever pot still was

built at Jameson's Distillery in Midleton, County Cork, in the nineteenth century.

The Smithfield site was home to the Bow Street Distillery of 1780, later renamed

John Jameson & Son, and it operated until 1971. The opening of the visitor centre

in 1997 went hand-in-hand with Dublin Corporation's plans to rejuvenate this

part of the city and encourage another financial services and residential centre to

balance the International Financial Services Centre east of the Custom House.

There is also another major attraction nearby: to the west is Collins

Barracks, where the National Museum has its Decorative Arts &

History displays.

THE GRAND CANAL BASIN

N ot many Dubliners would have been aware of the existence of Grand Canal Dock — or have even known where it was — before the DART line opened a railway station of that name not far away, between Pearse Street and Lansdowne Road stations. A few hundred yards of a walk will bring the commuter to the dock itself, a large, L-shaped sheet of water bisected in unequal parts by a traffic-bearing bridge, the smaller section nearer the station being a marina for old barges converted to modern use. The larger portion, partially seen in the foreground of our illustration, is nowadays used for recreational purposes, such as boating and water-skiing.

Together, the inner and outer docks formed one end of the Grand Canal, a waterway almost eighty miles long built between 1756 and 1805 to link Dublin with the River Shannon, and to provide both freight and passenger services. There is a striking picture by William Ashford in the National Gallery of Ireland celebrating the formal opening of the dock by Lord Camden, the Lord Lieutenant of the time. He stands beneath an outsize flag bestowing a knighthood on John Macartney, chairman of the company which built the canal. His gondola floats in seven metres of water at the foot of the wharf where the ceremony took place, with refreshment tents nearby, and a gun salute is fired from a nearby vessel. It certainly was an event worth celebrating, with three docks (only the central one of which is presently operational) to let boats in and out to the nearby River Liffey. This opened up long-distance, though slow, travel right across Ireland, from the Irish Sea to the Atlantic, until the advent of the railways in the middle of the nineteenth century curtailed its flourishing activity. Both the dock and the canal are now operated by Waterways Ireland, a joint North-South body that maintains and cares for the extensive range of canals throughout the island of Ireland.

Many of the vessels using the Grand Canal Dock in those days of yore were coal boats, and the men of Ringsend and Irishtown close by used to vie with one another for unloading jobs; only one man in three would be successful. Today, they are replaced by 'the madding crowd', mainly young but also old, out enjoying themselves on Grand Canal Square, including the modern jutting-out piece seen at the centre of the picture. The tents set back from the water – beside the commercial building on the left – are for the markets that take place occasionally here, adding to the square's excitement. The raised triangular buildings house air vents rising from an underground car park, and while they might seem out of character, they fit in remarkably well with the building taking up the centre of the background of the picture.

This is the Bord Gáis Energy Theatre, which started life in 2009 as the Grand Canal Theatre. It was designed to accommodate anything up to two thousand people, who come to view musicals and shows of the kind found in America and the West End of London, though there is also room for operas and other entertainments. Its creator is Daniel Libeskind, the Polish American 'starchitect' and theatre aficionado famous for the Jewish Museum in Berlin and the Ground Zero building in New York. He is one of a small band of well-known international architects who have helped to revitalise Dublin with extraordinarily imaginative buildings since the turn of the millennium, and Libeskind's theatre is undoubtedly one of the most memorable of these. Anyone who remembers Grand Canal Dock only twenty-five years ago will be amazed to see the change that has come over it since. All of the buildings seen here are products of the last ten, or at most twenty, years or so, with those in the background providing modern office accommodation for some of the city's largest law firms. The only exception is the old gasworks chimney peeping above the rooftops on the right, once associated with Dublin's famous gasometer, demolished to make way for the theatre.

The theatre roof slopes down towards the dock front, its

POSTMODERNISM

Postmodernist architecture, which became fashionable in the late 1970s, sought to introduce motifs from previous periods or features from the locality. The style later developed to include structurally interesting buildings such as the Bord Gáis Energy Theatre by the Polish American architect Daniel Libeskind. His work is not without its critics, but it could be said that Dublin has the best of Libeskind, since he designed this theatre on an almost-cleared site, with no need to work around existing buildings. Inside the theatre auditorium, the technical equipment is concealed by suspended 'sails', recalling the past of Dublin Port. The square's paving and planting scheme is by Martha Schwartz Associates.

Most of what we are seeing here is on ground reclaimed after 1711. Town gas was first produced in this area from 1824, supplying the street lights of Dublin. The gas industry became the major employer here, just as the railways predominated in other parts of the city. From 1986, natural gas came to Dublin, and this area lost its traditional businesses. Decontamination of the ground took from 1997 to 2002, and thereafter building began. Not far south of this view, an old gasometer received a new lease of life as the striking Gasworks apartments at South Lotts Road.

façade waving like a theatre curtain – the idea that inspired it. The area between the theatre and the dock is known as the 'Pole Park' because of the remarkable series of thin red poles standing seemingly random at an angle, reflecting the theatre-goers' enthusiasm as they spill outwards from the venue onto one of the city's largest open spaces. The poles, designed by Martha Schwartz Partners, light up at night, adding a festive, carnival atmosphere to the square for the evening strollers – a far cry from the gallows that gave the street leading up to it from the back the sinister name of Misery Hill. The more optimistic of the local inhabitants call the poles 'apple trees', because they believe an orchard once stood on the site. On the other side of Misery Hill is the Marker Hotel, opened in 2013, which dominates the right-hand side of the picture. Its undulating façade mirrors the gentle waves of Grand Canal Dock,

and it provides outside seating and tables warmed in the evening, with umbrellas for shade. The rooftop bar has a splendid view in all directions, including the south side of Dublin Bay as far as Dún Laoghaire.

The whole western end of Grand Canal Dock is a splendid example of how modern architecture can lift and revitalise a part of the city which had become almost derelict. Yet it was one small dock-side building along the tree-lined continuation of Hanover Quay – seen centre-right in the main image – that brought fame to the area during the last quarter of the twentieth century far beyond any of the more grandiose architectural creations of recent years. This came through the band U2 and their recordings made in the erstwhile Windmill Lane Studios, whose street-side wall was enriched with probably the densest collection of graffiti anywhere in Dublin or, indeed, the whole country.

A CANAL BARGE

A transformation occurs when you leave the Grand Canal Basin to start inland, following the canal as it begins its journey through south Dublin.

At Clanwilliam Place, all thoughts of the sea vanish and we are back in the city proper. With the tree-lined banks of the canal passing by Georgian

terraces along Warrington Place and Herbert Place, this is now an urban setting of a very high order. Barges glide along the waters. How different

this serenity must be from the days when the canal was a working thoroughfare.

The view here is towards McKenny's Bridge (originally Conyngham Bridge), named after Thomas McKenny, a director of the Grand Canal

Company in 1791.

TOWA
A NEW
HOR

The River Liffey, which divides Dublin north and south and links the city to the sea, rises in the Wicklow Mountains and flows down eighty miles before broadening out towards its mouth at the core of Dublin Port. Memories of the past are seen in the modern sailing ship the *Jeanie Johnston*, seen in the foreground of the detail opposite. It was called after a schooner built in Quebec in 1847 and bought by a Tralee man, Nicholas Donovan, who transported Irish emigrants on her during and after the years of the Great Famine of 1845–1847. It is appropriate that this horrific human disaster should be commemorated at the quayside just a little farther upstream by evocative statues of haunted-looking famine victims by the sculptor Rowan Gillespie, who erected them in 1997. Ten years later, his corresponding sculpture, *Migrants*, on the far side of the Atlantic, was unveiled in the Ireland Park in Toronto. In what is now the chq building nearby, a major 'visitor experience', entitled *Epic Ireland*, tells the story of the Irish diaspora spread throughout the world.

The ship which now bears the name *Jeanie Johnston* is not a copy of the original Canadian vessel; rather, it is based on a seventeenth-century Dutch East India ship, the *Batavia*, and was designed by Fred Walker, the chief naval architect with the Maritime Museum in Greenwich, England. Started in Blennerville near Tralee in County Kerry in 1993, it was finished nine years later, at a cost very much over the original estimate. It is built of larch planks on oak frames but, unlike its Dutch model, it is provided with engines and generators in case of emergency. It sailed to Canada and the United States in 2003 and has since made a number of further sea trips. But most of the time, it is

1. APARTMENT BUILDING WITH RESTAURANT BELOW

2. THE *JEANIE JOHNSTON*

3. HOTEL

4. THE CONVENTION CENTRE DUBLIN, ON THE SITE OF THE MID-
LAND GREAT WESTERN TERMINUS, WHERE CATTLE WERE UN-
LOADED FROM TRAINS FOR EXPORT ACROSS THE IRISH SEA

5. TWO SCHERZER BASCULE BRIDGES (RAISED BY USE OF A COUN-
TERWEIGHT) FROM CIRCA 1911, OVER THE ROYAL CANAL JUNC-
TION WITH THE RIVER LIFFEY

6. THE FORMER STATION OF THE LONDON AND NORTH WESTERN
RAILWAY COMPANY

7. THE HOTEL OF THE LONDON AND NORTH WESTERN RAILWAY
COMPANY, NOW OFFICES FOR IARNRÓD ÉIREANN

8. THE INTENDED ANGLO IRISH BANK HEADQUARTERS, ABAN-
DONED AFTER THE FINANCIAL CRASH OF 2008, NOW A NEW
HEADQUARTERS FOR THE CENTRAL BANK

9. FORMERLY THE PREMISES FOR LAIRD LINES' STEAMER SERVICES
BETWEEN SCOTLAND AND IRELAND

10. THE 3ARENA, A 14,500-CAPACITY AMPHITHEATRE. FORMERLY
GREAT SOUTHERN AND WESTERN RAILWAY GOODS STATION

11. FLOATING RESTAURANT THE *CILL AIRNE*

12. THE SAMUEL BECKETT BRIDGE

13. AREA OF THE ALEXANDRA BASIN, THE DEEP PORT WHERE ENOR-
MOUS CRUISE LINERS BERTH

14. POOLBEG LIGHTHOUSE

15. THE EAST-LINK BASCULE BRIDGE, OPENED 1984, THE LAST
BRIDGE OVER THE RIVER LIFFEY BEFORE DUBLIN BAY

16. THE DEEP CHANNEL THAT IS DREDGED TO MAINTAIN ACCESS TO
THE ALEXANDRA BASIN

17. WHARF AND WAREHOUSE ONCE USED BY TEDCASTLE,
MCCORMICK AND COMPANY, IMPORTERS/DISTRIBUTERS OF COAL

18. WHARF AND WAREHOUSE ONCE USED BY THE BRITISH AND IRISH
STEAM PACKET COMPANY (THE B&I)

19. A DIVING BELL DESIGNED BY THE ENGINEER BINDON BLOOD
STONEY, WHICH ENTERED SERVICE FOR DUBLIN PORT IN 1871
AND WAS USED UNTIL 1958

20. SIR JOHN ROGERSON'S QUAY

21. MARINA ON PIGEON HOUSE ROAD, OPPOSITE THE ENTRANCE
TO THE ALEXANDRA BASIN

22. TOP OF THE TWO TOWERS OF POOLBEG POWER STATION

moored alongside the quay, offering daily tours aboard by its owners, the Dublin Docklands Development Authority, who bought the vessel some years ago.

Up to half a century ago, one could have seen cattle being driven down the Quays for shipment to England, but these are now dung-clean and motorable to the car ferries — seen in the distance — and as far as Poolbeg generating station, with its iconic pair of tall towers, seen peeking over the buildings on the right as if guarding the entrance to the port.

The tall, tilted building farther along the quay from the *Jeanie Johnston* is the very striking Convention Centre, created by Kevin Roche, probably the most internationally renowned Irish architect of his generation. It opened in 2010, when he was eighty-eight years of age. Apprenticed to Michael Scott, another famous Irish architect fifteen years his senior, Roche became a pupil of Ludwig Mies van der Rohe in America, and was involved in the building of some of the most famous modern buildings in the United States, including the skyscrapers of the UN Plaza in New York. In recognition of his technical ingenuity and aesthetic style, he was awarded the Pritzker Prize, the highest award in his field, in 1982. On the laid-back shape of the Convention Centre, Roche was heard to quip that it reminded him of a glass of Guinness being drunk!

Farther along the north side of the Quays, there is a variety of buildings, hotels and offices in a modern style,

which have rejuvenated the quay-front. Where the hindmost set of cranes can be seen in the distance, there is a skeleton structure that was to be the new headquarters of Anglo Irish Bank, but the best laid plans of mice and men went awry during the financial crash in 2008, which put an end to the scheme, leaving a ghostly and ghastly unfinished presence on the Liffey's northern bank. However, all's well that ends well, and the Central Bank of Ireland has recently acquired the site, planning to make it into what it was intended to be, namely a bank headquarters, shown here in its finished state.

The whole centre of the picture is taken up with a much greater and more imaginative success story — the Samuel Beckett Bridge, named after Ireland's Nobel Prize-winning dramatist (1906–1989), author of *Waiting for Godot*, *Krapp's Last Tape* and other major contributions to the Theatre of the Absurd. Built in Holland, the bridge was towed all the way to Dublin in 2009 and has two lanes of traffic each way, with room for cycles and pedestrians; it connects Sir John Rogerson's Quay on the south side to Guild Street on the north, providing a fine view of the Conference Centre nearby. The bridge was designed by the Spanish architect Santiago Calatrava Valls, who also contributed another 'literary bridge' to the Liffey scene — the one named after James Joyce, farther upstream. Calatrava had the inspired idea of making the Beckett Bridge resemble the shape of a harp — Ireland's coat of arms – not upright but relaxed, lying on its back, with the 'strings' attached to a half-upright arm, forty-eight metres high, to support the 123-metre-long bridge. At the foot of the upright is a swivel mechanism, which allows the bridge to open and close, and the *Jeanie Johnston* and other craft to move effortlessly up and down the river.

This, however, was not the first swivel bridge the Liffey had seen. There was another one, just west of the present Butt Bridge, built by a man who had largely rebuilt the mid-eighteenth-century Essex Bridge and had broadened O'Connell Bridge for increased traffic. This was Bindon Blood Stoney (1828–1909), who was the most remarkable engineer ever to work for and in Dublin Port. His greatest achievement was the building of the Alexandra Basin, located roughly where the ferry boat is visible in the distance on the left bank of the river. This provided extra accommodation for larger craft, including the visiting cruise liners now coming into Dublin on an almost daily basis during the summer. Stoney built the basin through the use of 350-ton pre-cast concrete blocks, which he lowered into the water from a floating crane at one end of a boat with a weight on the other end to prevent capsizing. The blocks were placed in position underwater with the aid of a metal diving bell, in which the men could stay only for half an hour. For this invention he was awarded the Telford medal, and it made him an internationally recognised name in marine engineering circles. The whole story of this achievement is told in a quay-side exhibition on the south bank of the river a little below Calatrava's Samuel Beckett Bridge, displayed underneath the original orange-coloured bell, which has been preserved for posterity.

THE POOLBEG LIGHTHOUSE

Depending on the journey, this is either the first or the last landmark of Dublin's great port, reaching out miles into the bay — and not a place to go when the sea is angry. The first lighthouse was built here in 1767, and the present one dates from 1820. It is now automated and operated by the Dublin Port Company.

Silting was a problem for the port up to the eighteenth century, and measures had to be taken to improve accessibility for larger ships. The extraordinary achievement of the South Wall can be seen on maps from that time. At first, wooden piles were driven into the floor of the bay to create a barrier eastwards. These were not enough to withstand the fierce environment, and they were later strengthened by massive granite blocks hewn from the quarry at Dalkey. This gargantuan task was all in place by 1795. Large boats could tie up at the Pigeon House Harbour and unload their goods for transporting to Dublin by horse. The handsome, stone-built Pigeon House Hotel, dating from the 1790s, was intended for passengers arriving in heavier vessels. It is now offices and stands next to the redundant Poolbeg Power Station. In the decades to come, the hotel and surrounding area could become an arrival point for visitors in cruise ships, an echo of its original function.

SELECT BIBLIOGRAPHY

Includes edited volumes containing relevant articles not listed individually here.

Aalen, F.H.A. 'Approaches to the working-class housing problem in late Victorian Dublin: the Dublin Artisans Dwellings Company and the Guinness (later Iveagh) Trust.' *New research on the social geography of Ireland.* R.J. Bender (ed.). Mannheimer Geographische Arbeiten 17, 1984, 161–190.

Aalen, F.H.A. and Kevin Whelan (eds.). *Dublin city and county: from prehistory to the present.* Dublin: Geography Publications, 1992.

Almqvist, Bo and David Greene (eds.). *Proceedings of the seventh Viking congress, Dublin 15–21 April 1973.* Dublin: Royal Irish Academy, 1976.

Bennett, Douglas. *Encyclopaedia of Dublin.* Dublin: Gill and Macmillan, 1991.

Booker, Sparky and Cherie N. Peters (eds.). *Tales of medieval Dublin.* Dublin: Four Courts Press, 2014.

Borg, Alan. 'Theodore Jacobsen: a gentleman well versed in the science of architecture.' *Irish art historical studies in honour of Peter Harbison.* C. Hourihane (ed.). Princeton/Dublin: Four Courts Press, 2004, 276–294.

Bradley, John. *Viking Dublin exposed: the Wood Quay saga.* Dublin: The O'Brien Press, 1984.

Bradley, John, Alan J. Fletcher and Anngret Simms (eds.). *Dublin in the medieval world. Studies in honour of Howard B. Clarke.* Dublin: Four Courts Press, 2009.

Brady, Joseph. *Dublin, 1930–1950. The emergence of the modern city.* Dublin: Four Courts Press, 2014.

Brady, Joseph and Anngret Simms (eds.). *Dublin through space and time (c.900–1900).* Dublin: Four Courts Press, 2001.

Browne, Alan (ed.). *Masters, midwives and ladies-in-waiting: the Rotunda Hospital 1745–1995.* Dublin: A. & A. Farmar, 1995.

Bryan, Mary. 'Fitzwilliam Square.' *The Georgian squares of Dublin. An architectural history.* Dublin: Dublin City Council, 2006, 89–121.

Burke, Nuala. *Dublin's Wood Quay.* Drumconrath, Co. Meath: 1977.

Butler, Thomas C. *John's Lane: history of the Augustinian friars in Dublin 1280–1980.* Ballyboden: Good Counsel Press, 1983.

Campbell, Myles and William Derham (eds.). *The Chapel Royal, Dublin Castle. An architectural history.* Dublin: Office of Public Works, 2015.

Campbell Ross, Ian (ed.). *Public virtue, public love: the early years of the Dublin Lying-in Hospital: the Rotunda.* Dublin: The O'Brien Press, 1986.

Casey, Christine. *The buildings of Ireland. Dublin. The city within the Grand and Royal canals and the Circular Road with the Phoenix Park.* New Haven and London: Yale University Press, 2005.

Clarke, Desmond. *Dublin.* London: B.T. Batsford, 1977.

Clarke, H.B. *Dublin c.840 to c.1540: the medieval town in the modern city.* Dublin: Royal Irish Academy, 2002.

Clarke, H.B. *Dublin, Part I, to 1610. Irish Historic Towns Atlas No. 11.* Dublin: Royal Irish Academy, 2002.

Clarke, Howard, Sarah Dent and Ruth Johnson. *Dublinia. The story of medieval Dublin.* Dublin: The O'Brien Press, 2002.

Clarke, Howard (ed.). *Medieval Dublin. The making of a metropolis.* Blackrock, Co. Dublin: Irish Academic Press, 1990.

Clarke, Howard (ed.). *Medieval Dublin. The living city.* Blackrock, Co. Dublin: Irish Academic Press, 1990.

Clarke, Howard B. *The four parts of the city: High life and low life in the suburbs of medieval Dublin. The Sir John T. Gilbert Commemorative Lecture, 2001.* Dublin: Dublin City Public Libraries, 2003.

Clarke, Howard B., Máire Ní Mhaonaigh and Raghnall Ó Floinn (eds.). *Ireland and Scandinavia in the early Viking Age.* Dublin: Four Courts Press, 1998.

Clarke, Howard B. and Ruth Johnson (eds.). *The Vikings in Ireland and beyond: before and after the Battle of Clontarf.* Dublin: Four Courts Press, 2015.

Clarke, Howard B., Jacinta Prunty and Mark Hennessy (eds.). *Surveying Ireland's past: multidisciplinary essays in honour of Anngret Simms.* Dublin: Geography Publications, 2004.

Coffey, George and E.C.R. Armstrong. 'Scandinavian objects found at Island-Bridge and Kilmainham.' *Royal Irish Academy proceedings* 28C, 1910, 107–122.

Conlin, Stephen. *Historic Dublin: from walled town to Georgian capital.* Dublin: The O'Brien Press, 1986.

Conlin, Stephen (with Jonathan Bardon). *One thousand years of Wood Quay.* Dublin: The O'Brien Press, 1984.

Cooke, Pat. *A history of Kilmainham Gaol 1796–1924.* Dublin: Stationery Office, 1995.

Cosgrave, Art (ed.). *Dublin through the ages.* Dublin: College Press, 1988.

Costello, Murray and Beaumont. *An Introduction to the Royal Hospital, Kilmainham: its architecture, history and restoration.* Dublin: Published by the authors, 1987.

Costello, Peter. *Dublin churches.* Dublin: Gill & Macmillan, 1989.

Costello, Peter. *Dublin Castle in the life of the nation.* Dublin: Wolfhound Press, 1999.

Craig, Maurice. *Dublin 1660–1860.* Dublin: Hodges Figgis, 1952.

Crawford, John. *Within the walls: the story of St. Audoen's Church, Cornmarket, Dublin*. Dublin: St. Patrick's cathedral group of parishes, 1986.

Crawford, John and Raymond Gillespie (eds.). *St. Patrick's Cathedral, Dublin: a history*. Dublin: Four Courts Press, 2009.

Curran, C.P. *The Rotunda Hospital: its architects and craftsmen*. Dublin: The Three Candles Press, 1945.

Curran, C.P. 'The architecture of the Bank of Ireland.' *The Bank of Ireland 1783–1946*. F.H. Hall (ed. George O'Brien). Dublin: Hodges Figgis/Oxford: Blackwells, 1949, 423–471.

Curran, C.P. *Dublin decorative plasterwork of the seventeenth and eighteenth centuries*. London: Alec Tiranti, 1967.

Curtis, Maurice. *The Liberties: a history*. Dublin: The History Press, 2013.

Daly, Mary, Mona Hearn and Peter Pearson. *Dublin's Victorian houses*. Dublin: A. & A. Farmar, 1998.

Daly, Mary E., *Sixties Ireland: reshaping the economy, state and society, 1957–1973*. Cambridge University Press, 2016.

De Courcy, John, with drawings by Stephen Conlin. *Anna Liffey, the river of Dublin*. Dublin: The O'Brien Press, 1988.

De Courcy, John W. 'The Liffey Banks in Dublin. The early works of the private developers.' *Dublin Historical Record* 57(2), 2004, 146–151.

Dickson, David. *Dublin. The making of a capital city*. London: Profile Books, 2014.

Dillon, William A. 'The Tailor's Hall, Back Lane.' *Quarterly bulletin of the Irish Georgian Society* 3(2), April–June 1960, 9–12.

Dixon, F.E. 'The Dublin Tailors and their Hall.' *Dublin Historical Record* 22(1), 1968, 147–159.

Donnelly, N. *Short histories of Dublin parishes*. Dublin: The Catholic Truth Society, 1905–1912 (reprinted Blackrock, Co. Dublin: Carraig Books, 1977).

Donnelly, P.J. *Remains of St. Mary's Abbey. Their explanations and researches A.D. 1886*. Dublin: Forster & Co., 1887.

Doran, Gráinne. 'Smithfield Market – past and present.' *Dublin Historical Record* 50(1), 1997, 105–118.

Dudley, Rowena. 'St Stephen's Green: the early years, 1664–1730.' *Dublin Historical Record* 53 (1), 2000, 157–179.

Duffy, Seán (ed.). *Medieval Dublin*, I, 2000 – XV, 2016. Dublin: Four Courts Press.

Gillespie, Elgy (ed.), *The Liberties of Dublin*. Dublin: E & T O'Brien, 1973.

Goodbody, Rob. *Dublin, Part III, 1756–1847. Irish Historic Towns Atlas 26*. Dublin: Royal Irish Academy 2014.

Griffith, Lisa Marie. *Stones of Dublin: a history of Dublin in ten buildings*. Cork: The Collins Press, 2014.

Grimes, Brendan. *Majestic shrines and graceful sanctuaries. The church architecture of Patrick Byrne 1783–1864*. Dublin and Portland, Oregon: Irish Academic Press, 2009.

Guinness, Desmond. *Georgian Dublin*. London: B.T. Batsford, 1979.

Gwynn, Aubrey. 'The origins of St. Mary's Abbey, Dublin.' *Journal of the Royal Society of Antiquaries of Ireland* 79, 1949, 110–125.

Gwynn, Aubrey and R.N. Hadcock. *Medieval religious houses. Ireland*. London: Longmans, 1970 (reprinted 1988).

Halpin, Andrew. *The port of medieval Dublin: archaeological excavations at the Civic Offices*. Dublin: Four Courts Press, 2000.

Heffernan, Thomas Farel. *Wood Quay: the clash over Dublin's Viking past*. Austin, Texas: University of Texas Press, 1988.

Historic Area Rejuvenation Plan (HARP). Dublin: Dublin Corporation c.1998.

Hughes, Andrew. *Lives less ordinary: Dublin's Fitzwilliam Square 1798–1922*. Raheny, Co. Dublin: Liffey Press, 2011.

Igoe, Vivien. *Dublin burial grounds & graveyards*. Dublin: Wolfhound Press, 2001.

Johnson, Ruth. *Viking Age Dublin*. Dublin: Town House, 2004

Kelly, Merlo. *An introduction to the architectural heritage of Dublin north city*. Dublin: Department of Arts, Heritage and the Gaeltacht, 2015.

Laffan, William and Brendan Rooney. '"I have treated you as an artist": a letter from Philippe–Jacques de Loutherbourg to Jonathan Fisher.' *Irish architectural and decorative studies* 17, 2014, 40–49.

Lalor, Brian. *Ultimate Dublin guide. An A–Z of everything*. Dublin: The O'Brien Press, 1991.

Lang, James T. *Viking Age decorated wood*. National Museum of Ireland. Medieval Dublin excavations 1962–1981. Ser. B., Vol. 1. Dublin: Royal Irish Academy, 1988.

Lee, Clive (ed.) with Patricia McCarthy. *Surgeon's halls. Building the Royal College of Surgeons in Ireland 1810–2010*. Dublin: Royal College of Surgeons, 2011.

Lennon, Colm. *Dublin, Part II, 1610–1756. Irish Historic Towns Atlas No. 19*. Dublin: Royal Irish Academy, 2008.

Lennon, Colm. 'The great explosion in Dublin, 1597.' *Dublin Historical Record* 42, 1988–89, 7–20.

Lennon, Colm and John Montague. *John Rocque's Dublin. A guide to the Georgian city*. Dublin: Royal Irish Academy, 2010.

Loeber, Rolf, Hugh Campbell, Livia Hurley, John Montague and Ellen Rowley (eds.). *Art & architecture of Ireland, Vol. IV, Architecture*. New Haven/London: Yale University Press, 2014.

Lord Mayor's bye-laws for the regulation of Smithfield Market and of all other hay, straw and cattle markets within the Borough of Dublin. Dublin: 1854.

Luddy, Ailbe J. *St. Mary's Abbey, Dublin*. Dublin: M.H. Gill, 1935.

McCarthy, Patricia. 'A favourite study.' *Building the King's Inns*. Dublin: Gill & Macmillan, 2006.

McCartney, Donal. *U.C.D. A national idea. The history of University College, Dublin*. Dublin: Gill & Macmillan, 1999.

McCullen, John. *An illustrated history of the Phoenix Park. Landscape and management to 1880*. Dublin: Government Publications, 2009.

McCullough, Niall. *Dublin: an urban history*. Dublin: Associated Editions/Lilliput, 1989.

McCutcheon, Clare. *Medieval pottery from Wood Quay*. National Museum of Ireland. Medieval Dublin excavations 1962–81. Ser. B, Vol. 7. Dublin: Royal Irish Academy, 2006.

McDonnell, Joseph. 'Cramillion, Bartholomew.' *Art and architecture of Ireland, Vol. III, sculpture 1600–2000*. Paula Murphy (ed.). New Haven/London: Yale University Press, 2014, 83–84.

McGrail, Seán. *Medieval boat and ship timbers from Dublin*. National

Museum of Ireland. Medieval Dublin excavations 1962–81. Ser. B., Vol. 3. Dublin: Royal Irish Academy, 1993.

MacLaran, Andrew. *Dublin, the shaping of a capital.* London and New York: Belhaven Press, 1993.

McLoughlin, Adrian. *Guide to historic Dublin.* Dublin: Gill & Macmillan, 1979.

MacMahon, Mary. *St. Audoen's Church, Cornmarket, Dublin: archaeology and architecture.* Archaeological Monograph Series: 2. Dublin: Stationery Office, 2006.

McManus, Ruth. *Dublin 1910–1940: shaping the city and suburbs.* Dublin: Four Courts Press, 2002.

McParland, Edward. 'The Wide Street Commissioners: Their importance for Dublin architecture in the Late 18th – Early 19th century.' *Quarterly bulletin of the Irish Georgian Society* 15(1), January–March 1972, 1–32.

McParland, Edward. 'The buildings of Trinity College, Dublin.' *Country Life* 4114 (6 May 1976) 1166–69; 4115 (13 May 1976), 1242–45 and 4116 (20 May 1976), 1310–13.

McParland, Edward. *James Gandon. Vitruvius Hibernicus.* London: Zwemmer, 1985.

McParland, Edward. 'The Royal Hospital, Kilmainham, Co. Dublin.' *Country Life* 4577 (9 May 1985), 1260–63 and 4578 (16 May 1985), 1320–24.

McParland, Edward. *Public architecture in Ireland 1680–1760.* New Haven and London: Yale University Press, 2001.

Maguire, J.B. 'Seventeenth century plans of Dublin Castle.' *Journal of the Royal Society of Antiquaries of Ireland* 104, 1974, 5–14.

Malcomson, A.P.W. *Nathaniel Clements, 1705–77. Politics, fashion and architecture in eighteenth-century Ireland.* Dublin: Four Courts Press, 2015.

Maxwell, Constantia. *Dublin under the Georges.* London: Faber and Faber, 2nd revised edition, 1946.

Meehan, Bernard. 'A fourteenth-century historical compilation from St. Mary's Cistercian abbey, Dublin.' *Medieval Dublin XV,* 2016, 264–276.

Meredith, Jane. *Around and about the Custom House.* Dublin: Four Courts Press, 1997.

Milne, Kenneth. *The Dublin Liberties, 1600–1850.* Maynooth Studies in Local History 82. Dublin: Four Courts Press, 2009.

Milne, Kenneth (ed.). *Christ Church Cathedral, Dublin: a History.* Dublin: Four Courts Press, 2002.

Moody, T.W. and F.X. Martin. *The course of Irish history.* Cork: Mercier Press, 1967 (and several later reprints).

Murphy, Margaret and Michael Potterton. *The Dublin region in the Middle Ages. Settlement, land-use and economy.* Dublin: Four Courts Press, 2010.

Murray, Hilary. *Viking and early medieval buildings in Dublin.* Oxford: British Archaeological Reports, British Series 119, 1983.

New history of Ireland (various eds.). Vols. I–IX, 1976–2005. Oxford: Clarendon Press.

Ní Ghradaigh, Jenifer and Emmett O'Byrne (eds.). *The march in the islands of the medieval west.* Leiden/Boston: Brill, 2012.

Numbers 8–10 Henrietta Street. Dublin: Dublin Civic Trust, 2003.

O'Byrne, Anne M. *Bartholomew Mosse: a physician who accomplished his dream.* Bethesda, Maryland: Wild Apple Press, 2014.

O'Dwyer, Frederick. *Lost Dublin.* Dublin: Gill & Macmillan, 1981.

Ó Grada, Diarmuid. *Georgian Dublin: the forces that shaped a city.* Cork: Cork University Press, 2015.

Ó Muirí, Seán Antóin. *Dublin architecture. 150+ buildings since 1990.* Kinsale: Gandon Editions, 2014.

O'Reilly, Seán and Alistair Rowan. *University College, Dublin.* The Irish Heritage Series 68. Dublin: Eason, 1990.

O'Sullivan, Niamh. *Every dark hour: a history of Kilmainham Jail.* Dublin: Liberties Press, 2007.

Pearson, Peter. *The heart of Dublin. Resurgence of an historic city.* Dublin: The O'Brien Press, 2000.

Pearson, Peter. *Peter Pearson's decorative Dublin.* Dublin: The O'Brien Press, 2002.

Simms, Anngret. 'Medieval Dublin: a topographical analysis.' *Irish Geography* 12, 1979, 25–41.

Simpson, Linzi. 'Forty years a digging: a preliminary synthesis of archaeological excavation in medieval Dublin.' *Medieval Dublin* I, 2000, 11–68.

Somerville–Large, Peter. *Dublin.* London: Hamish Hamilton, 1979.

Twomey, Brendan. *Smithfield and the parish of St. Paul, 1698–1750.* Maynooth Studies in Local History 63. Dublin: Four Courts Press, 2005.

Vaughan, W.E. (ed.). *The Old Library, Trinity College, Dublin 1712–2012.* Dublin: Four Courts Press, 2013.

Viking and medieval Dublin. National museum excavations 1962–1973. Catalogue of exhibition. Dublin: Árd-Mhúsaem na h-Éireann, 1973 (reprinted 1976).

Viking settlement & medieval Dublin. Dublin: Curriculum Development Unit, 1978.

Wallace, P.F. 'Dublin's waterfront at Wood Quay: 900–1317.' *Waterfront archaeology in Britain and Northern Europe.* Gustav Milne and Brian Hobley (eds.). Council for British Archaeology Research Report 41. London: Council for British Archaeology, 1981, 109–118.

Wallace, P.F. *The Viking Age buildings of Dublin.* National Museum of Ireland. Medieval Dublin Excavations 1962–81. Ser. A, Vol. 1, parts 1 and 2. Dublin: Royal Irish Academy, 1992.

Wallace, Patrick F. *Viking Dublin. The Wood Quay excavations.* Sallins, Co. Kildare: Irish Academic Press, 2016.

Walsh, Claire. *Archaeological excavations at Patrick, Nicholas and Winetavern streets.* Dingle: Brandon Press/Dublin Corporation, 1997.

Watson, Elizabeth. *St. Andrew's Church, Westland Row, Dublin. 'An enduring presence.'* An overview of the history of St. Andrew's Church from its origins to the present. Dublin: c.2007.

Wilde, William. 'Biographical memoir of Bartholomew Mosse, M.D., surgeon and licentiate in midwifery and founder of the Dublin Lying–in Hospital.' *Dublin Quarterly Journal of Medical Science for November* 1846, II, 565–596.

Williams, Jeremy. *A companion guide to architecture in Ireland, 1837–1921.* Blackrock, Co. Dublin: Irish Academic Press, 1994.

Wyse Jackson, Patrick. *The building stones of Dublin.* Dublin: Country House, 1993.